Antennas & TV Program Guide

Reviews, comparisons, and step-by-step instructions

By Ken Wickham

I0488766

Antennas + TV Program Guides
ISBN-13: 978-1499321135
ISBN-10: 1499321139
 Kindle ASIN: B00K1M63SK

First Edition : May 15, 2014

Updated First Edition : February 2, 2015

14 13 12 11 10 / 10 9 8 7 6 5 4 3 2 1

Dedication

This book is dedicated to all the antenna suppliers, video streamer devices, low priced subscription services, and free online media content providers

Thank You.

Ken

Forthcoming in this series

Internet + Wi-Fi phones

FTA Satellite

Also Available

Streaming Devices + Streaming Services
ISBN-13: 978-1500399276
ISBN-10: 1500399272
Kindle ASIN: B00KWO3P6K

Antennas & Streaming
SBN-13: 978-1500399986
ISBN-10: 1500399981
Kindle ASIN: B00KWPCS9Y

Table of Contents

Notes concerning Updated First Edition:

Really, I have only made 3 changes.

1) I added 4k TV specs to the resolution list. 2) I also added a really good method that I enjoy to the rabbitears.info methods which I now call the Best Quick Easy Overall Method because it shows the sub channels, unlike most of the other methods. It saves having to do multiple steps. 3) I expanded the links found in the back of the book to the different cable, satellite, and network television stations.

One advantage to also buying a digital version of this book, I will update the digital version prior to doing a physical book update. This is because ebooks are easier to update the files. I don't have to worry so much about details such as page format and appearance.

This book, I call the updated February 2, 2015 First Edition of <u>Antennas + TV Program Guides</u>. I did not make enough changes in the rest of the book to warrant a 2nd edition.

Ken Wickham

Author

February 2, 2015

Sick of expensive unused channels

$157 monthly. $1884 annually.

That's how much money we were paying for cable television and internet. Sure we had 300+ channels. However, how many did we actually use?

How many of the paid channels do you use?

We watched two singing contest shows, a few suspense thrillers, a comedy sitcom, and a couple of sci-fi series. We actually only watched four TV shows at any given time, due to different show seasons. Occasionally, we rented a movie from the big red colored box outside store, or ordered through the mail some rental movie internet video from a monthly subscription. We did this because we didn't want to wait a year to watch these just-out-of-the-theater movies.

I noticed quickly, that the movies we received from the premium channels, we had already seen through the box, received via the mail or online streaming. There was only one premium TV show series that we watched 3 months every year.

How many TV shows come from network broadcast television?

Most of the TV shows we watched came from network broadcast television. Only three cable television series came from the part of cable that we paid. The portion that we paid for premium cable was about $100, only to watch three shows, and an occasional interesting history or biography documentary. That is $1,200 a year for three shows plus a few shows here and there.

Rise of the Cord Cutters

Sick of paying all this money for almost nothing, I had to think of an alternative. Many have cut their cable bills entirely off and become what many call "cord cutters".

Companies that have an eye towards the future are heading this wave of personalized-on-demand, subscription, or free commercial paid content.

Netflix, Google, Hulu, Amazon and even a few cable and satellite such as Xfinity, Dish Network, and DirecTV are companies are heading towards mobile, and more personalized content. TV Broadcasters are filling their websites with streaming episodes and content. A few live streams of news and a few networks already are on the net.

TV media devices are quickly becoming a part of everyday life

Remember antenna television

I remembered the time when all of my television was free coming from broadcast transmission towers received by a television antenna. We had rabbit ears sometimes modified with hangers and tinfoil, and sometimes one of those loop antennas for UHF.

After the digital conversion a few years ago, I was unsure if we could pick up any channels or how.

We watched several shows on the net anyway

Whenever we missed shows we realized that many networks would put some of their shows online, normally the last two to five episodes. We used this method to watch our favorite shows that we missed or hadn't seen because we were watching something else at that scheduled time. Normally the episodes appear on the network sites the next day.

Flash forward to where I am now

My mother and step-father are living north of Denver Colorado 50 miles. They have been spending $137 monthly for cable television. Analyzing what they actually watch, I told them I could save them maybe $80 at least a month and still receive most of the content that they watched every day. That's about $1000 a year in savings. They watch the news, health shows, reality contest shows, alien visitation documentaries, and ancient archeology documentaries and series. They also liked to listen to relaxation music.

I asked if they had an antenna.

My father-in-law said he did, and eventually found them in storage. I hooked them up one night and scanned for channels. Forty-two channels appeared.

2-1 KWGN - DT - The CW
2-2 KWGN – DT2 - This TV
4-1 KCNC – DT - CBS
5-1 KGWN – DT – CBS
5-2 KGWN – DT2 – Northern Colorado 5
5-3 KGWN – DT3 – The CW
6-1 KRMA-DT – PBSHD
6-2 KRMA - DT2 – V-ME
6-3 KRMA – DT3 - Create
14-1 KTFD - DT – Telefutura
14-2 KTFD – DT2 – Bounce
14-3 KTFD – DT3 - GetTV
20-1 KTVD – DT - MyNet

20-2 KTVD – DT2 MeTV

22-1 KFCT - DT - FOX

22-2 KFCT – DT2 – Antenna TV

24-1 CTVa – EWTN

24-2 TorahTV

24-3 Oorah

24-4 Impacto

27-1 KLWY – DT - FOX

27-2 KLWY – DT2 – ABC (KTWO rebroadcast)

31-1 KDVR – DT - FOX

31-1 KDVR – DT2 – Antenna TV

33-1 KQCK – DT – MundoFOX

36 Analog - Azteca

38-1 KPJR – DT - TBN

38-2 KPJR – DT2 – ChurchChannel

38-3 KPJR – DT3 – JuiceTV

38-4 KPJR – DT4 – TBNEnlace

38-5 KPJR – DT5 - Smile

44-1 KDNF – DT – Daystar

47-1 KRMA-DT – PBSHD

47-2 KRMA - DT2 – V-ME

47-3 KRMA – DT3 - Create

50-1 KCEC – DT - Univision

50-1 KCEC – LATV – LATV

59-1 KPXC - TV – ION

59-2 KPXC - TV2 - Qubo

59-3 KPXC – TV3 – IONLife

59-4 Shop

59-5 HSN

We started watching the over-the-air (OTA) antenna TV content for the next few days. After these few days of watching antenna television, my step-father made a call to his cable content provider to cut off his cable service entirely. I told him to keep the internet service. The Cable charged him large early disconnect fee, but we knew in the long run we would be saving money.

Apartment, indoor antenna

I live in an apartment currently 50 miles north of Denver. Because I live in an apartment, the rules prohibit attaching to the building. Indoor antennas are a necessity in this situation. My step-father had an amplified rabbit ears and convertor box already. What about places in the middle of nowhere?

In the middle of nowhere near Canadian border

I lived in Antler, North Dakota for a month last year. Although we received paid TV. I wondered what channels would even reach there, way out in the middle of nowhere. Here is what is listed. Of course, one would need an outdoor, rooftop, or tower antenna.

With a good roof antenna, my brother in Antler, ND, very near the US-Canada Border can pick up most major network broadcasts. CBS, NBC, FOX, ABC, PBS, World Channel, MN Channel, PBS Encore, Weather, Me-TV.

And with a repositioning north he might be able to pick up 3 Canadian channels which would give the two Canadian networks CTV and GTN.

Moderate Signal   **KXMC** CBS   *13-1*   *Hi-V*

Channel	Aspect	Format	Programming
13.1	16:9	1080i	main KXMC-TV programming / CBS
13.3	4:3	480i	Weather

Moderate Signal   **KMOT** NBC   *10-1*   *Hi-V*

Channels	Aspect	Format	Programming
10.1 / 8.1	16:9	1080i	Main KMOT/KUMV programming / NBC
10.2 / 8.2	4:3	480i	Me-TV

Weak Signal   **KSRE**   PBS   *6-1*   *UHF*

Channel	Video	Audio	Call Sign	Network/Programming	Nickname	Notes
06-1	40.3		1080i	DD2.0 PPB1 PBS	"Prairie Public Television"	
06-2	40.4		480i	DD2.0 PPB2 World Channel		
06-3	40.5		480i (w)	DD2.0 PPB3 MN Channel	"Minnesota Channel"	
06-4	40.6		480i	DD2.0 PPB4 PBS Encore	"Lifelong Learning"	

Weak Signal   **KXND**   FOX   *24-1*   *UHF*

Channel	Video	Audio	Call Sign	Network/Programming		Nickname	Notes
24-1	24.3		720p	DD5.1 KXND-DT	FOX	"Fox 24"	

Weak Signal   **KMCY** ABC   *14-1*   *UHF*

Channel	Video	Audio	Call Sign	Network/Programming		Nickname	Notes
14-1	14.3		720p	DD2.0 KMCY-HD	ABC	"KMCY 14"	

And Possibly Canadian TV Channels

Very Weak Signal CKYB CTV 4, CKND GTN 2, CIEW CTV 7

Summary of Antenna Setup Instructions

Before you are able to receive and use over-the-air broadcast signals, you must take a few steps to plan, purchase the needed equipment and accessories, set everything up, and set up useful TV program guides.

These steps begin with analyzing your TV which leads you to three tools that can help you figure out the possible over-the-air content you might be able to receive. A list of possible antenna and accessory retailers and online stores is given. The book then gives some universal steps to setting up your channels.

1. [ ] If you don't have an antenna and only a TV first write down the qualities of your TV or computer monitor you will be watching your TV. This information includes connector types, TV tuner, and screen resolution. Record this info on the planning information sheet in section I. You may print off a copy of the planning pages.

2. [ ] Next, use the online tools to figure out signal tower directions, distances, and signal strength. For more information how to use these tools read the *TV Transmission Tower Information* chapter. Record this info on your planning pages in the appropriate section in section II

3. [ ] Also, complete the Channel Information sections to figure out the available channels, networks, and sub channels using the available tools explained also in that same chapter. If two or more of the same channel are broadcast from different towers, there is room enough to record the two closest towers. Record this information in section III in the planning pages.

4. [ ] With this information you should have a good idea what content is available over-the-air. You will also be equipped with the information needed to purchase an antenna.

5. [ ] Using the information compiled and written down from step 2 and knowledge of possible signal blocking obstacles, you can purchase the appropriate antenna. Use the information in *What Kind of Antenna Do I Need* chapter.

6. [ ] Scout for retail antennas, online antennas, or professional installers. See the list of possible places that sell antennas at the back of the book. Consult a local antenna installer if you need help installing a roof antenna. Learn the return policies just in case things don't work out as planned. Purchase the best antenna for your planned situation within your budget. Keep all receipts in case things don't work out as planned.

7. [ ] Install or have someone with the required skills install your antenna. Indoor antennas should be easy enough to do on your own or by someone with basic antenna knowledge. The antenna coaxial cable should go in the antenna input of the TV tuner. If you have an old TV, converter boxes then have an output which hook up to the TV.

8. [ ] Set up your TV to scan for channels.

9. [ ] Set up a *TV Program Guide* to help you plan upcoming content.

10. Enjoy!

Planning your TV entertainment services

TV Antenna

In the book or on separate pieces of paper, please write down the following information in order to help you setup an alternative to expensive paid TV

I. What type of television connectors does your TV have? How many?

- Coaxial _____
- HDMI _____
- S-Video _____
- Compodite (LR(red white) audio, (yellow) video _____
- Component (Green - Y, blue – Pb, red – Pr; all three are video, audio is separate)
- USB _____
- VGA _____
- DVI _____

What kind of TV tuner will you be using? (Check or write down each one)
  A. Built in TV   [ ]
  B. TV converter box   [ ]
  C. Computer TV tuner   [ ]

What is your TV resolution?
  A. 480i (analog) [ ]
  B. 480p (digital) [ ]
  C. 720p [ ]
  D. 1080p [ ]
  E. WQHD 1440p [ ](Highest currently possible)

II. What general direction are the transmission towers? [FCC Method] (Write Direction]

- Strong signals (Green) _____

  _____

- Moderate signals (Yellow) _____

  _____

- Weak signals (Orange) _____
- No signals (Red) _____

How many stations are: Low-V(HF)_____, Hi- V(HF)_____, UHF_____?

What is the exact direction and distance to the towers? [TVFool.com Method]

Channel Real - Virtual - Network - Distance - Direction - True - Magnetic

_____ _____ _____ _____ _____ _____ _____

_____ _____ _____ _____ _____ _____ _____

Channel Real - Virtual - Network - Distance - Direction - True - Magnetic

III. What Networks are listed? [Use Rabbitears.com Method] (check or write down each one)

Networks

CBS [ ] Chan _____Dir_____Dist_____ || Chan _____Dir_____Dist_____

ABC [ ] Chan _____Dir_____Dist_____ || Chan _____Dir_____Dist_____

NBC [ ] Chan _____Dir_____Dist_____ || Chan _____Dir_____Dist_____

Fox [ ] Chan _____Dir_____Dist_____ || Chan _____Dir_____Dist_____

CW [ ] Chan _____Dir_____Dist_____ || Chan _____Dir_____Dist_____

ION [ ] Chan _____Dir_____Dist_____ || Chan _____Dir_____Dist_____

Qubo [ ] Chan _____Dir_____Dist_____ || Chan _____Dir_____Dist_____

IONLife [ ] Chan _____Dir_____Dist_____ || Chan _____Dir_____Dist_____

Public

PBS [ ] Chan _____Dir_____Dist_____ || Chan _____Dir_____Dist_____

Create [ ] Chan _____Dir_____Dist_____ || Chan _____Dir_____Dist_____

World [ ] Chan _____Dir_____Dist_____ || Chan _____Dir_____Dist_____

MHZ Worldview [ ] Chan _____Dir_____Dist_____ || Chan _____Dir_____Dist_____

NHK World (Japan) [ ] Chan _____Dir_____Dist_____ || Chan _____Dir_____Dist_____

France24 (French, English, Arabic) [ ] Chan _____Dir_____Dist_____

V-Me (Spanish) [ ] Chan _____Dir_____Dist_____ || Chan _____Dir_____Dist_____

Shows and Movies

ThisTV [ ] Chan _____Dir_____Dist_____ || Chan _____Dir_____Dist_____

GetTV [ ] Chan _____Dir_____Dist_____ || Chan _____Dir_____Dist_____

AntennaTV [ ] Chan _____Dir_____Dist_____ || Chan _____Dir_____Dist_____

MeTV [ ] Chan _____Dir_____Dist_____ || Chan _____Dir_____Dist_____

MyNetwork [ ] Chan _____Dir_____Dist_____ || Chan _____Dir_____Dist_____

BounceTV [ ] Chan _____Dir_____Dist_____ || Chan _____Dir_____Dist_____

CoziTV [ ] Chan _____Dir_____Dist_____ || Chan _____Dir_____Dist_____

RetroTV [ ] Chan _____Dir_____Dist_____ || Chan _____Dir_____Dist_____

Movies! [ ] Chan _____Dir_____Dist_____ || Chan _____Dir_____Dist_____

Music

Zuus Country [ ] Chan _____Dir_____Dist_____ || Chan _____Dir_____Dist_____

CoolTV [ ] Chan _____Dir_____Dist_____ || Chan _____Dir_____Dist_____

Mens

Tuff TV [ ] Chan _____Dir_____Dist_____ || Chan _____Dir_____Dist_____

Weather

Accuweather [ ] Chan _____Dir_____Dist_____ || Chan _____Dir_____Dist_____

WeatherNation [ ] Chan _____Dir_____Dist_____ || Chan _____Dir_____Dist_____

Local Weather [ ] Chan _____Dir_____Dist_____ || Chan _____Dir_____Dist_____

American One [ ] Chan _____Dir_____Dist_____ || Chan _____Dir_____Dist_____

TV Guide
TV Scout [ ] Chan _____Dir_____Dist_____ || Chan _____Dir_____Dist_____
Shopping
QVC [ ] Chan _____Dir_____Dist_____ || Chan _____Dir_____Dist_____
HSN [ ] Chan _____Dir_____Dist_____ || Chan _____Dir_____Dist_____
JewelryTV [ ] Chan _____Dir_____Dist_____ || Chan _____Dir_____Dist_____
Religious
TBN [ ] Chan _____Dir_____Dist_____ || Chan _____Dir_____Dist_____
Daystar [ ] Chan _____Dir_____Dist_____ || Chan _____Dir_____Dist_____
Enlace (Spanish) [ ] Chan _____Dir_____Dist_____ || Chan _____Dir_____Dist_____
Smile of a Child [ ] Chan _____Dir_____Dist_____ || Chan _____Dir_____Dist_____
JuiceTV [ ] Chan _____Dir_____Dist_____ || Chan _____Dir_____Dist_____
The Church Channel [ ] Chan _____Dir_____Dist_____ || Chan _____Dir_____Dist_____
3ABN [ ] Chan _____Dir_____Dist_____ || Chan _____Dir_____Dist_____
Cornerstone [ ] Chan _____Dir_____Dist_____ || Chan _____Dir_____Dist_____
EWTN [ ] Chan _____Dir_____Dist_____ || Chan _____Dir_____Dist_____
FamilyNet [ ] Chan _____Dir_____Dist_____ || Chan _____Dir_____Dist_____

Spanish
Univision [ ] Chan _____Dir_____Dist_____ || Chan _____Dir_____Dist_____
Telemundo [ ] Chan _____Dir_____Dist_____ || Chan _____Dir_____Dist_____
MundoFox [ ] Chan _____Dir_____Dist_____ || Chan _____Dir_____Dist_____
UniMas [ ] Chan _____Dir_____Dist_____ || Chan _____Dir_____Dist_____
Estrella TV [ ] Chan _____Dir_____Dist_____ || Chan _____Dir_____Dist_____
Azteca America [ ] Chan _____Dir_____Dist_____ || Chan _____Dir_____Dist_____
LATV [ ] Chan _____Dir_____Dist_____ || Chan _____Dir_____Dist_____
Existos TV [ ] Chan _____Dir_____Dist_____ || Chan _____Dir_____Dist_____
Zuus Latino [ ] Chan _____Dir_____Dist_____ || Chan _____Dir_____Dist_____
Health and Wealth
Living Well Network [ ] Chan _____Dir_____Dist_____ || Chan _____Dir_____Dist_____
Biz Television [ ] Chan _____Dir_____Dist_____ || Chan _____Dir_____Dist_____

What type of antenna do you have (will you get)? (circle which one is best)
Indoor unamplified (unblocked, less than 25 miles from transmission tower): Urban and Suburban. Forms- flat, rabbit ears, and loop. Great value if unblocked by trees, buildings, and near towers.
Indoor amplified (booster) (unblocked, less than 40 miles from transmission tower): Near rural areas, suburban, urban. Forms- similar to unamplified except with a plug in for the amplifier.

Attic amplified (less than 45 to 50 miles from transmission towers): Form basically a small enough outdoor antenna, instead mounted on a poll or pillar in the attic. You may need to construct some basic mount or pole depending on your attic.

Outdoor amplified (unblocked, normally less than 70 miles from transmission tower) Rural areas, near rural areas, suburban, urban. These can be

Breadth and depth (circle which one is best)

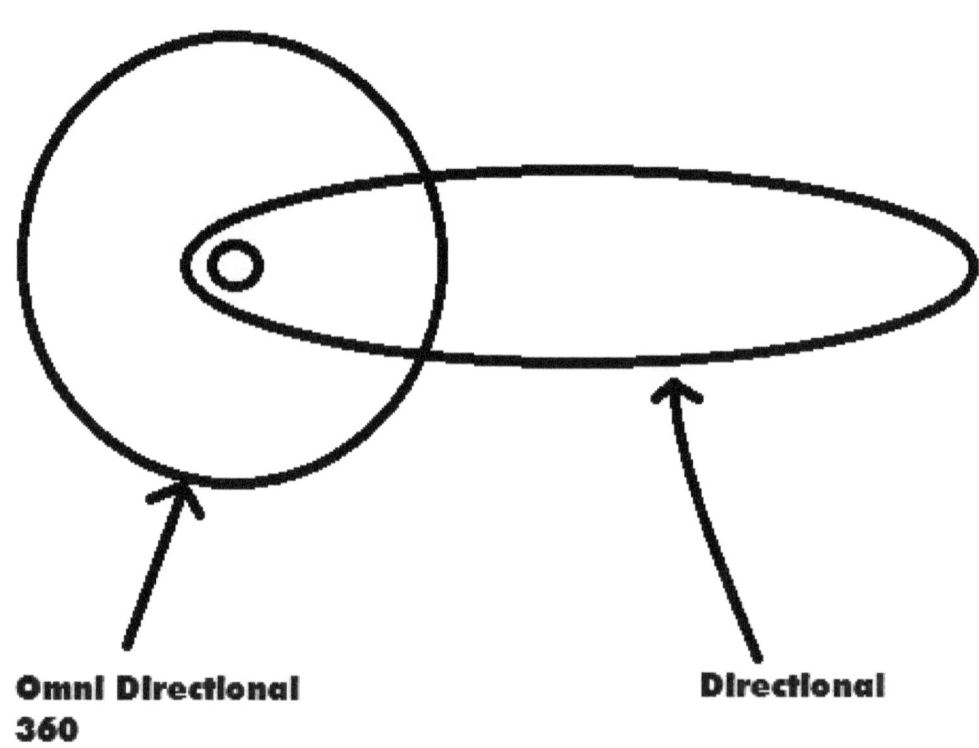

Omni Directional 360

Directional

General arc of two major types of TV antennas
Ranges are not drawn to scale

Drawing for illustrative purposes only. The range and shape are not entirely accurate. See professional specifications for actual shape and range of each antenna and type. By Ken Wickham

Omnidirectional (360degrees): In the center of multiple towers surrounding under 40 mile range.

Multi-directional: an antenna that picks up signals for a wider angle, 50 to 90 degrees, though it loses some distance vs directional. Distance however is further than 360 degree antennas

Directional fixed: Signals coming from one direct, within (20 degrees best, 35 degree limit of each other).

Rotatable (rotor): Benefits of directional antenna range, though you can rotate the antenna to aim at different directions. Signals coming from all around you. Less than 70 miles from transmission.

Pick a TV Program Guide

[ ] The built-in TV EPG guide is sufficient.

[ ] TVListings.AOL.com

[ ] TitanTV.com

[ ] TVGuide.com

[ ] Zap2It.com

[ ] TV.com

The first thing I bought for my first antenna setup in Mississippi was a nice amplified indoor antenna. We lived near a medium populated city, and did not need a roof or attic antenna. I chose a *Micron-R ClearStream Micron Indoor UHF DTV Antenna with Reflector Screen*. After hooking the antenna on, plugging in the amplification power adaptor, and doing a channel antenna search, only a few fuzzy channels appeared. I realized this was an older television needing an analog to digital convertor box. My mother-in-law used one of these boxes connected to her roof antenna to get television out in the farming country region. We bought a TV signal analog to digital converter box, hooked it up, and tried a channel search. The specs showed only a 35 mile range, though we pulled in signals from 40 miles away with a little adjustment of the direction and adding a booster.

What Kind of Viewing TV or Computer Tuner do you own?

The first step you need to do figure out if your TV has a built in digital TV tuner, or is an older analog TV tuner. If you are going to use a computer as a TV you will need to check if you have a TV tuner card (normally indicated by a coaxial input port on your computer.

Built into TV [ ]
Converter Box [ ]
Tuner Card [ ]

At the same time, you may want to make a list of all the devices you plan on including in your entertainment system.

Accessories
Antenna [ ]
Media Player [ ]
Media Streamer [ ]
DVR [ ]
DVD player [ ]
Blue-ray player [ ]
Video game console [ ]
Sound system or speakers [ ]

TV Connectors
Next, you need to know what type of connectors are included on your television(s) you will be using.

Common TV Connectors

HDMI

HDMI emerging in 2004, HDMI has replaced coaxial as the high definition connection of modern televisions. 90% of HDTVs by 2007 had HDMI connectors. By 2009, all digital televisions had at least one HDMI connectors. Many converters exist to convert different type of connectors and wires into HDMI. The signal probably will not play at the highest resolution however. Be cautious of having too many connectors, splitters, and wires which leads to signal loss and overall masses of wire octopuses.

S-Video

S video has a max 480i/576i signal definition. S-Video is slightly better than composite video, using 2 channel encryption instead of one. You may have to use this for older TVs though composite a/v is normally more common.

Composite A/V

Older TVs might need to use the composite port. Composite has a max of 480i/576i. This is the 3 color wires of yellow for video, and red and white for audio. Composite A/V is slightly lower quality compared to S-Video because it only uses one channel instead of the two that S-Video uses.

Ethernet

Cat-5e is the current standard for Ethernet wiring. Ethernet wiring is mainly used to connect devices by wire to routers and modems.

Coaxial

Older still is the basic coaxial input and output. RG-6 is the current standard for coaxial cable.

USB

USB port on TVs can run movies, listen to music, and look at pictures from a thumb drives. It can also update the TVs firmware by downloading the software putting it on a thumb drive then inserting the drive into the port. External hard drives can also be used to play content connecting directly to the TV.

TV resolution, aspect ratio, formats

When the entire United States switched over from analog to digital service, the entire country was thrown into a little frenzy. What emerged however has its advantages and disadvantages.

The old analog signal was a continuous updating signal. The further and weaker the signal, you might still be able to get a fuzzy picture with some sound. The digital signal is more of an all-or-nothing type signal. This means you either get it or don't. Although in reality, you can get some channels that are pixelated. Normally those pixelated channels you can tune in with proper repositioning of the antenna, change of height, or addition of a booster (amplifier).

Modern signal types

Broadcaster digital terrestrial television (DTV) broadcasting. Broadcasters normally transmit one or both types of picture formats, which vary in size and aspect-ratio. High definition television (HDTV) for the transmission of high-definition video and standard-definition television (SDTV).

The i and p in the resolution

In the signal transmission the gap is called *interlacing video* (symbol = i) in the analog method and progressive (symbol = p). In interlacing they sent half a frame at a time, first the odd lines then the even lines. Now they send line-by-line. So when you read 720p, this actually means 1280x720 digital *progressive scan* signal in that it receives a signal line by line. This reduced eyestrain from interline twitter making images and movement more smooth.

Old analog signals (for comparison)

CGA computer monitors had a resolution of 320x200 up to 640x200 4 bit 16 color.

VGA computer monitors (1987) introduced 640x480 up to 800x480 16 bit in 4:3 aspect ratio. VGA has 256 colors in 320x200 mode. The second resolution is the VHS and Betamax resolution. 480i is also the broadcast resolution of old analog televisions.

Current HDTV signals

HD 480p has 640x480 pixel or 4:3 aspect ratio (4 units wide by 3 units high) is SDTV. This is closest to DVD quality which is 720x480 which can be shrunk to fit SDTV, or play in widescreen mode with dark space above and below the picture.

HD 720p widens the resolution to 1280x720 16:9 aspect ratio.

HD 1080p resolution of 1920 × 1080 at a 60 Hz with 16:9 aspect ratio. This is Blue-ray resolution.

4K resolution of 3840 x 2160 with 16:9 aspect ratio. This is also called Ultra-high-definition television (UHDTV). YouTube, Netflix, and Amazon stream content now in this resolution.

What Kind of Antenna Do I Need

With the information gathered from primarily TVFool.com and the FCC, you can begin to process of choosing an antenna. Special focus is given to your range, the signal RF channels, and the compass direction of the towers.

Estimating antenna range by type

A rule-of-thumb general estimate of range of TV Antenna is 70 miles for **outdoor antennas** with ideal conditions due to the curvature of the earth. Using an indoor antenna generally cuts the signal in half, so 35 miles is a general range rule for **indoor antennas**. Some VHF signals with proper conditions may pick up signals 100 miles away. UHF (majority of signals) have a much shorter range. A basic rabbit ears **unamplified** is good for about 10 miles.

What type of signal frequencies are you trying to receive (UHF v VHF or UHF&VHF)?

The FCC, TVFool.com, and Rabbitears.com tell the RF, Physical, or true channel that the signal transmits using. Also they tell the Virtual, Display channel. Use the RF channel to figure out how many real VHF channels you have. Most channels will be UHF.

VHF

VHF covers the frequencies channel range of 2 to 13. Channels 2 through 6 are Low Band VHF channels. Channels 7 to 13 are High Band VHF channels.

UHF

UHF covers the frequency channels 14 to 51. UHF frequencies advantage is that there normally isn't as many interfering signals due to devices, computers, and other noise.

Will you focus the signal on one direction or need multi direction or all-around signal reception?

Directional – Benefit is longer range. Disadvantage is narrower width of signal reception.

Fixed – Antenna is facing one direction. Advantage is if all signals come from one direction and have a narrow width.

Rotatable – Antenna can move around. You gain the advantage of having a directional long range antenna. However, you can rotate the antenna to pick up multiple directions. Thus you create a 360 degree long range antenna ability.

Multi-Directional – Means somehow it can receive signals from more than one direction. Depending on the type of multi-directional it may or may not receive signals 360 degrees.

Omnidirectional – You can receive signals from any direction barring obstacles. Disadvantage is you will have a shorter range. This type of antenna is great if you are surrounded by many signal towers that are not that far away like when you are in a city.

Will you be able to place the antenna outdoor, in the attic, or will it be indoor room only?

Most of the signal tools in this book will list signal strength by colors green representing indoor antenna, yellow represents attic antenna, and orange represents outdoor antenna needed.

Do you need any amplification (booster)?

In my experience an amplification can help gain channels that you can only partially or barely receive. You will not gain a ton of channels, rather you might be able to pick up a few don't come in clear. Amplifiers also amplify noise, which could make some channels worse. Too much gain causes overload.

You should get an antenna with the accessories that give you a little more gain than you need. Excessive gain leads to overload. Too little gain will lead to inability to receive the enough signal.

Long coaxial cable runs might require a pre amp or amplifier. Use of splitters might require use of amplifiers.

TV signal reception

The old television analog needed less of a signal strength for reception than digital. In addition, in analog, the signal frequency identified the channel. Most channels now broadcast on Ultra High Frequency (UHF) band which are line of sight (LOS) and do not go around or through signals. They may or may not be identified by their radio frequency (RF channel). Some are identified by their DTV or virtual channel designation rather than their actual RF channel. When scanning for channels, you will see the channels accepted using the RF channel number. When you actually change the channel using the remote, it will show up using the DTV channel number, if different from the actual RF channel.

What do I need to look for in a TV tuner?

ATSC

ATSC is the signal standard for North America which replaced the most of the old analog signal standard NTSC in the US on June 12, 2009. ATSC means Advanced Television Systems Committee.

Note on other signal types standards

You will probably come across several different standards for signal transmission.

NTSC

NTSC is the old signal standard and signal standard for analog TV used primarily before June 12, 2009. A few analog channels still exist. NTSC means National Television System Committee.

QAM (DVB-C)

QAM is the digital cable standard. QAM means quadrature amplitude modulation. The signal is called DVB-C, also meaning Digital Video Broadcasting — Cable.

DVB-S is the digital satellite standard. DVB means Digital Video Broadcasting — Satellite.

What about older TVs?

TVs made before accepting the new ATSC TV standard will require a TV *converter box*. The converter box, instead of the set channel changer, will control the changing of the channels. The set is normally set on 3, 4, or some sort of input source mode. Read the instructions of the converter box for details. The converter box wired between the antenna (coaxial IN) and the TV (coaxial, HDMI, or component out).

Normally a wireless remote controls the channels and volume. Programmable remotes can replace lost or damaged remotes, or consolidate several remotes for several devices.

What do I need to turn my computer or laptop into a TV?

Computers require a TV tuner in order to receive TV signals, also some sort of software is needed to display the TV channels. Look for a TV tuner that can receive ATSC signals. Also you will need the drivers, which come on a DVD disk. Modern windows can automatically searches for the drivers, if you are connected to the internet. In Microsoft Windows you can use Windows Media Center to play live TV. Mac uses Front Row as its Media Center main software.

My computer TV tuner

TV Antenna types

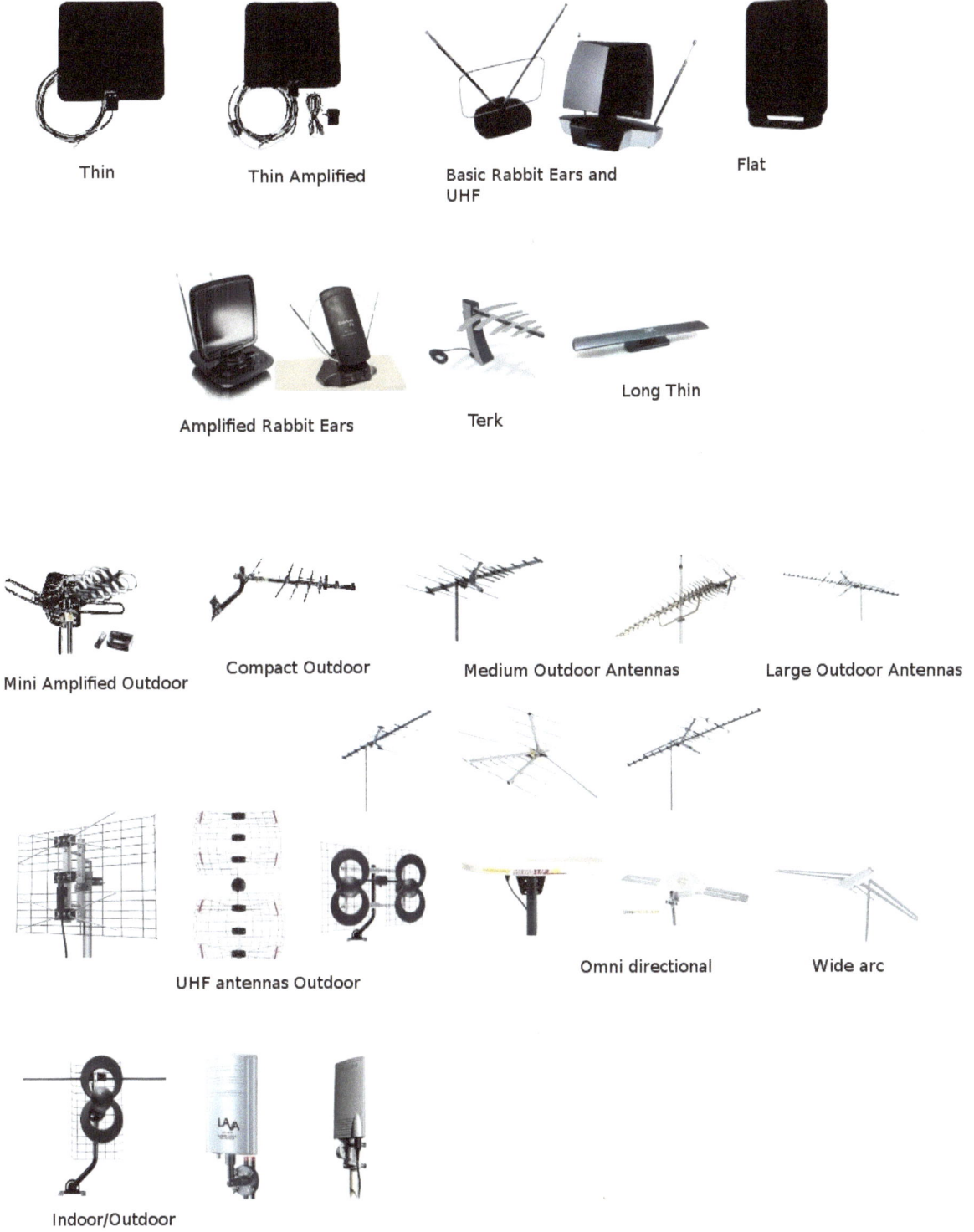

This chart for comparison purpose shows the variety of types one can make depending on the type of TV antenna needed.

Making a TV Antenna

We following these instructions and made a great antenna higher gain than the amplified indoor antenna that we bought.

"How to get HD channels with a $2 homemade antenna" by John Matarese posted 9:16 AM, Feb 11, 2014. http://www.abcactionnews.com/money/consumer/dont-waste-your-money/how-to-get-hd-channels-with-a-2-homemade-antenna

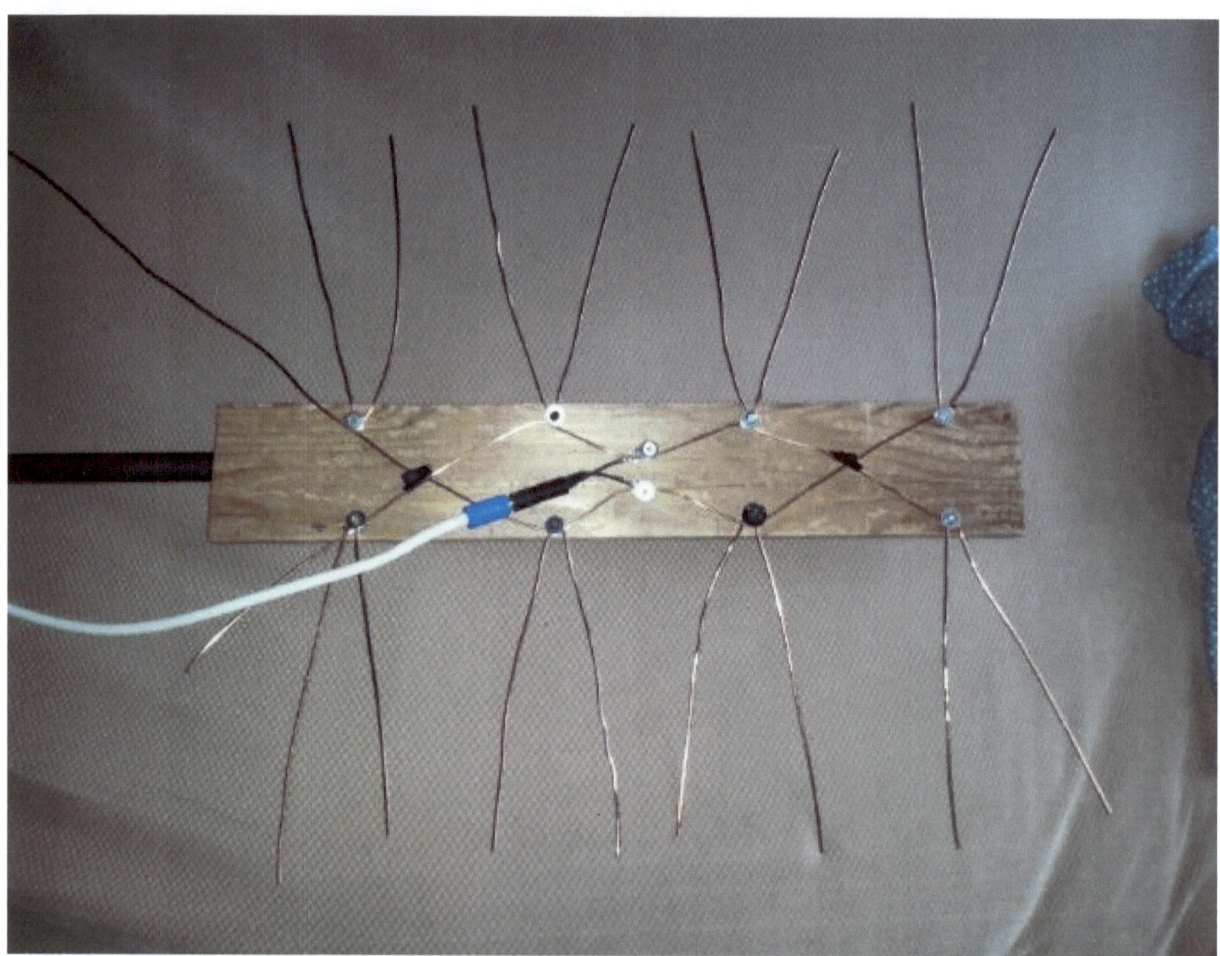

Notes on TV accessories

Wire

Coaxial cable – the wire that connects antennas to the TV. For TV antennas, RG-6 is the common wire type. RG- 59 is for satellite systems. The longer the coaxial runs, the weaker the signal. Short coaxial runs with no or few connections or splits would result in the best signal connection.

Color of wires

White – Normally used indoor along trims, since most indoor rooms are white or very light.

Black – Normally used in walls and outdoors.

75 ohm coaxial RG – 6 is the standard for TV antennas that replaced the old 300 ohm twin lead (flat wide looking wire). Older antennas on older homes may still have the old wire. If so attach a 300 ohm to 75 ohm Matching Antenna Balun Transformer and then run a new line of coaxial RG – 6

Solid wire cores

Good – Standard coaxial - cable copper coated steel wire.

Better – Solid copper coaxial cable (though more expensive)

Shielding

Shielded or regular – Shielded is normally indicated by Quad-shielding. Regular only has one or two shields

Other Ratings

Flooded/Direct Burial – This coaxial can be buried under ground in conduit. Flooded has a sticky outer coating to help protect it from the moisture.

Outdoor cable also have a UV rating.

UL Ratings

CMP – Plenum – installing in ducts, fire resistant, low smoke and toxin producing.

CMR – Riser – used to prevent spread of fire in elevator shafts from floor to floor.

CM – Used to prevent fire in areas other than plenum or risers.

Coaxial **F-type connectors**

Worst - Twist on

Better – Crimp on. Look for outdoor water resistant with O-rings and sealing gel

Best – Compression fittings

Ground – Outdoor antenna masts need to be grounded with #8 or #10 copper or aluminum wire directly to a copper coated steel ground rod 3 feet deep at least. The wire should be attached to the mast directly good and solid, scrapping off paint if necessary (then painting or sealing over the connected ground). There should be no more than 90 degree turns and turns should be gradual and smooth. Do not attach to pipes or plumbing.

Splitters & Combiners

Splitter – Takes one input and divides the signal into two or more outputs. The higher the quality, the less the signal loss. All splitters divide signals weakening the signal strength. The less the number of divisions and connections the better the signal.

High Bandwidth Splitter – Used to split higher bandwidth of HDTV like 1GHz or 2GHz

Combiner – Takes two input sources (ex 2 antennas) and combines the signals into one output.

Splitter/Combiners – These can be used as either a splitter or a combiner.

Amplifiers – Amplifiers come in two major types. Pre Amps and Signal Amplifiers
Pre Amp - used for coaxial runs longer than 50 feet or when towers are 45 miles or greater distance.

Signal Amplifier – Amplifiers can be used sometimes integrated with combiners and splitters. Or it can be used to recover lost signal after a splitter.

Outdoor antenna mount types

Tripod (roof peaks)
Eave mount kit
Chimney
Wall
J-Pole

When mounting on a roof or wall, ensure that

Rotors – Rotators – Mast mounted motor allowing the antenna to orient towards different directions via an indoor control.

Don't place outdoor antennas near power lines.

Don't bend coaxial too sharply

Apply silicon grease or acrylic insulator to older antennas connections with a Balun transformer.

Four Free Online Tools to Get Antenna Range, Distance, Sub channel, Network Information

A) TV Transmission Tower Information

What general direction are the transmission towers? (Easy Quick Method)

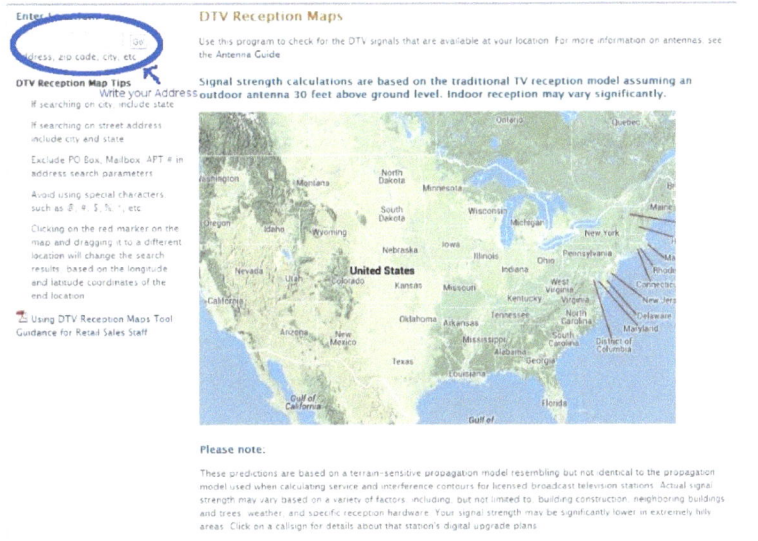

Where to type your address.

FCC Digital TV Maps

http://transition.fcc.gov/mb/engineering/dtvmaps/

1. Enter your address into the location box circled in blue.
2. After entering your address **enter** or click on the **GO** button.
3. Signal strength is show primarily color coded.
   a. The call signs shaded in green you should easily be able to pick up with an indoor antenna, unless some obstacle impedes your signal such as a hill or large building. Amplification or booster may increase some channel reception.
   b. Yellow means you may need an attic antenna.
   c. Orange you need an outdoor roof antenna.
4. The Network is the primary station network. Other networks and digital subchannels can be contained within each channel broadcast which you will find using the Rabbitears tool.
5. Note the band. The band helps you to determine which type of antenna you need. How many Low-V, Hi-V, UHF

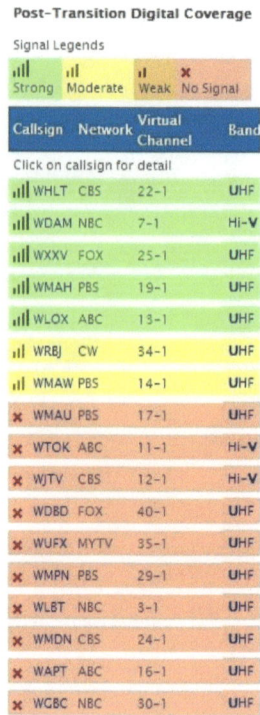

A quick FCC check on channels shows this for Hattiesburg, MS. This is all the major networks

6. Click on each callsign to see expanded information for that tower. Additional information show will be as followed.
    a. A location on the map will be show. You can zoom in and out to better see the location of the TV tower transmitter.
    b. The virtual channel number and the RF channel broadcasted.
    c. The receiving power in dBm. The combination of antenna, and amplifiers, minus the cord length, distance loss, obstacle interference, splitter loss must equal above zero to be able to view the channel.
    d. A compass direction and general direction. In addition the location will be shown on the map.
    e. You can click on the **Gain/Loss Map** link to see a map of the viewing area.
7. For now just write down the call signs and general direction for stations that come up green, yellow, orange, and red. Your main focus now will be to figure out which directions are most important. Are there any repeat stations in different directions? If so, the one in the dominant direction might be more important and easier to receive.

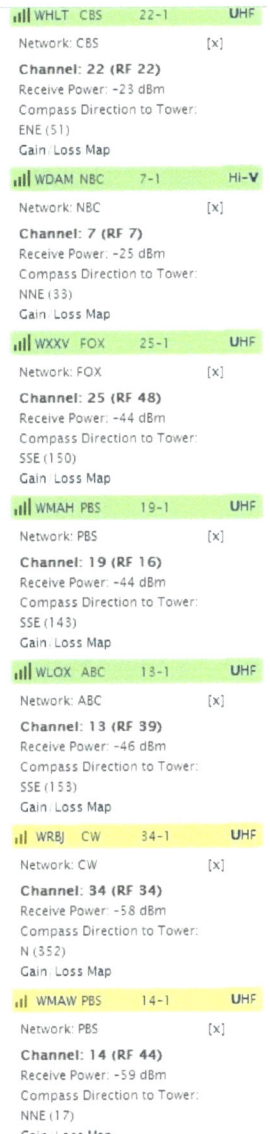

Checking the map of the main signals shows the directions of the transmission towers. As you can see most of the channels are either NE, NNE or SSE. I see where these transmission towers are by clicking on each of the network call letters. So these are the main direction focus.

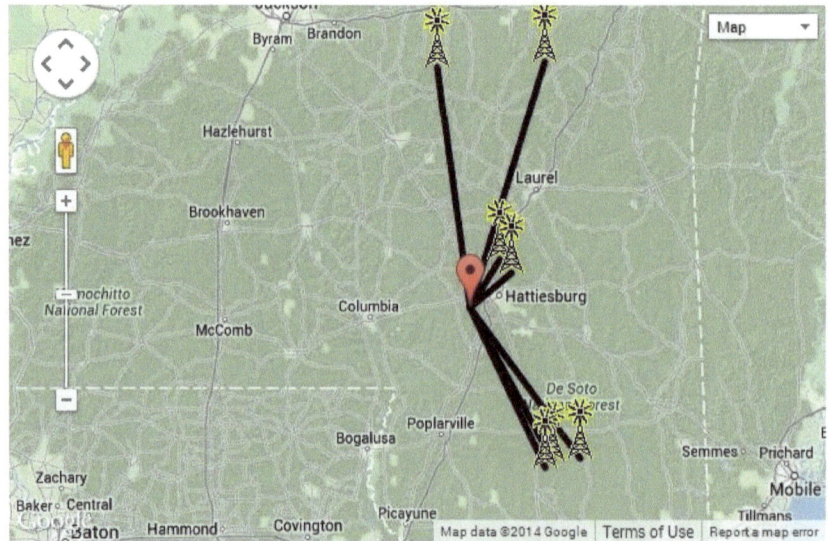

The channels on the list above come from the 60 mile range. Only two transmission towers are 14 miles away; NBC and CBS. Three are 40 miles away; PBS, FOX, and ABC. Two are 60 miles away; CW and another PBS. You can see on the map above the direction of these towers, I get the exact distance from another tool that I will mention from TVFool.com.

No Signal Transmission Towers

Just to know if I get adventurous, where are these red channels coming from. I click on these to find out, while deselecting the ones I probably will get. Mostly NW and W are the channels that would be less likely to reach my house in Hattiesburg. One comes from the NNE. These channels are about 90 miles away according to TVFool.com.

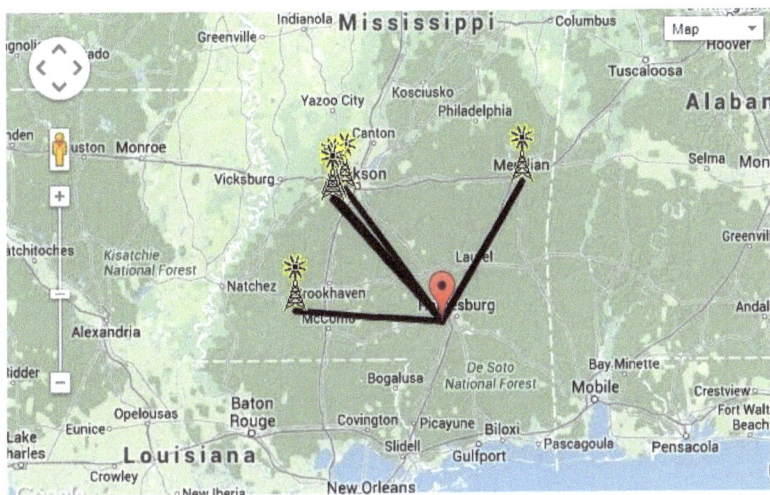

Another Example

For a quick peak you can go to http://transition.fcc.gov/mb/engineering/dtvmaps/ and enter your address. You may or may not be able to pick up the channels on this fast list. This list assumes you have a 30 foot high antenna without any obstacles. If you have an indoor antenna or have buildings and hills in the way, you may not get some of these channels. You can click on the station callsign on this list to see which direction the signal is originating from.

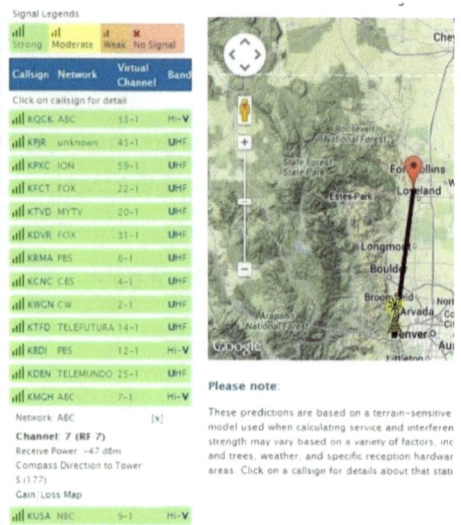

One of the signal towers impeded by buildings.

Example: When trying it for my area it shows 20 call signs or networks. 6 of them, however we do not pick up. Further analysis shows that these channels originate from a direction where 4 huge buildings block. Also important to note, 3 of these channels are repeats of the same network from different antennas. So of the 20 possible channels we can pick up, 6 are blocked by buildings, and three are repeated twice. So in total 11 unique network call signs are listed in this list.

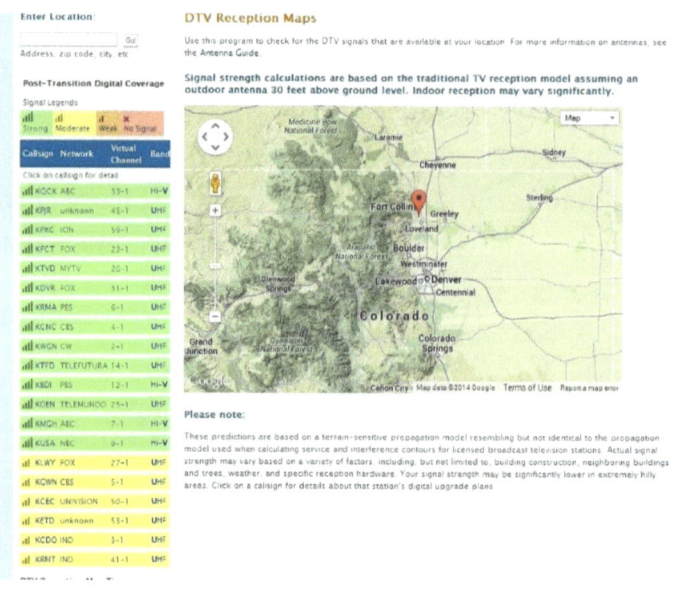

DTV Reception Maps FCC

http://transition.fcc.gov/mb/engineering/dtvmaps/

B) AntennaWeb.Org (CEA certified outdoor antennas EZ Method)
http://www.antennaweb.org/

The Consumer Electronics Association (CEA) and the National Association of Broadcasters (NAB) built this website to better select outdoor TV antennas. Their certified antennas are based on a seven color zone system. They don't really cover indoor antennas.

I am a bit weary of this information. The results that said I need a powerful rooftop antenna, I can receive with an indoor amplified antenna. The information may be old.

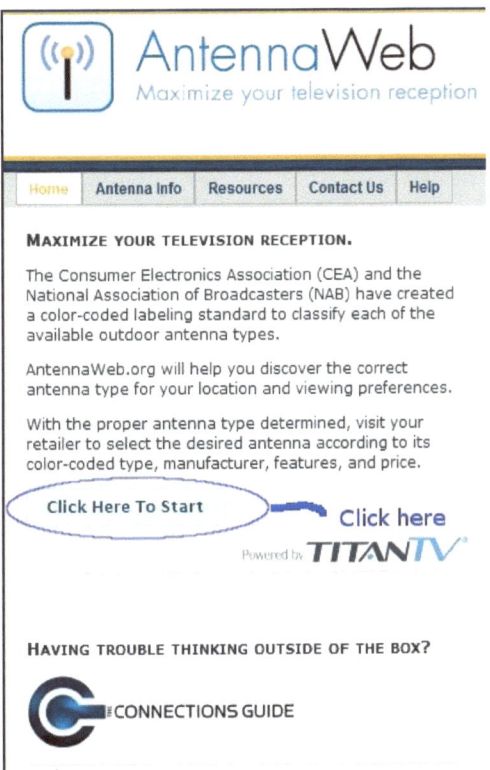

1. Click on *Click Here to Start.*
2. Enter your *ZIP code* in the box.
3. I recommend you put your address in the *Street Address* section. The first time I tried using just the ZIP gave me only 4 channels. Entering my ZIP code resulted in 12 channels.
4. AntennaWeb.org is mainly geared towards external roof antennas. 30 feet high and above is the ideal height for outdoor antennas. Select *"Yes"* if this is the height that your antenna will be mounted. Select *"No"* if it will be lower.
5. Click Submit, after you have entered the ZIP, Address, and antenna height.

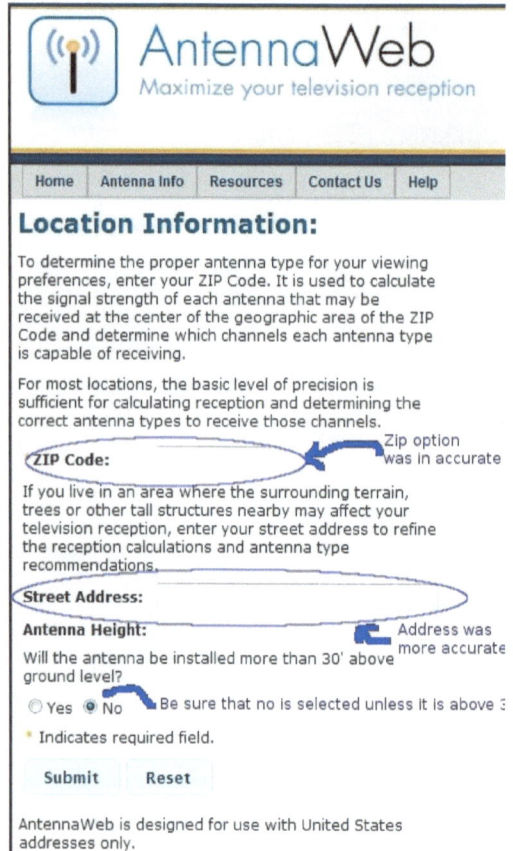

Antennaweb.org classifies the six types of outdoor antennas
*(Information from Antennaweb.org **Antenna Info** page)*

Yellow: Small multi-directional antennas – The smallest TV antenna receiving signals 360 degrees. They may be disks and patch shaped antennas or attached to satellite systems. Use in high signal areas. Yellow - 10 to 15 mile range.

Green: Medium Multi-directional – These are a bit larger and more powerful antennas that receive signals 360 degrees. These antennas may be stick, wing, or disk shaped antennas with long elements. Use this antenna when 20 foot or more runs are needed. Also if you will attach more than one device. Green - Up to 30 mile range.

Light Green: Large Multi-directional – Big size. Receives more signal power at a greater distance. Element antennas used to reject ghost situations. Light Green - Up to 30 mile range

Light Green: Small Directional - multi – This antenna is an element rooftop antenna. Light Green - Up to 30 mile range.

Yellow. Green, Light Green, Red, and Blue: Medium Directional – The most popular antenna. Multi-elemental. Amplified versions allow blue zone coverage. Red – up to 45 miles. Blue - Up 45 to 60 miles.

Green, Light Green, Red, Blue, Violet: Large Directional – Large antennas used in weak signal areas. Multi-elemental. Amplified versions allow blue and Violet color zone coverage, though will eliminate yellow zone coverage. Violet - 60 miles or more.

Where to get CEA certified antennas.

The two web stores partnering with the CEA color zone code antenna systems are:

http://www.channelmaster.com/

http://www.antennacraft.net

C) What is the distance to these transmission towers, power of these transmissions, and exact compass heading? (More Exact, Time Consuming, and Accurate Method)

Next we can figure out the distance to most of the transmission towers as well as the exact direction for compasses. We need to know the distance to help us figure out more exact what kind of TV antenna we need. TV fool.com does a great job in helping us our here. Under 25 miles, you can get away with antennas that are not amplified. Over 25 miles, amplified antennas are more desirable.

1. Go to www.tvfool.com
2. Click on **TV Signal Locator** button.

3. Enter your address and height of antenna or where you plan to put the antenna. You can search several times at different heights to see how the height will affect your signal reception.

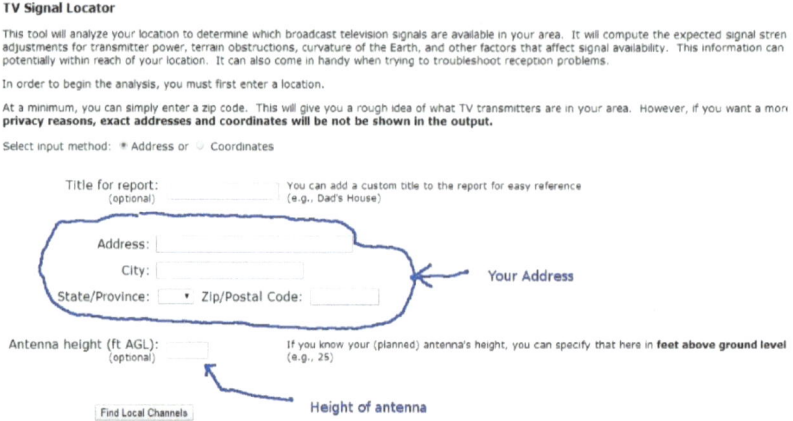

4. This method shows more information concerning signal strength, distance, and path. In addition they provide a 360 degree showing the directions of the RF channel of the towers and relative strength.

5. The All Channels channel listings on the bottom VHF Lo, VHF Hi and UHF channel lineup and strength shows the channels according to their RF channels. This VHF and UHF channel listing also shows possible conflicting channels and relative strength of each.

6. Write down the more detailed information for the channel info that you gathered from the FCC quick method concerning: real, virtual, network, distance, and direction.

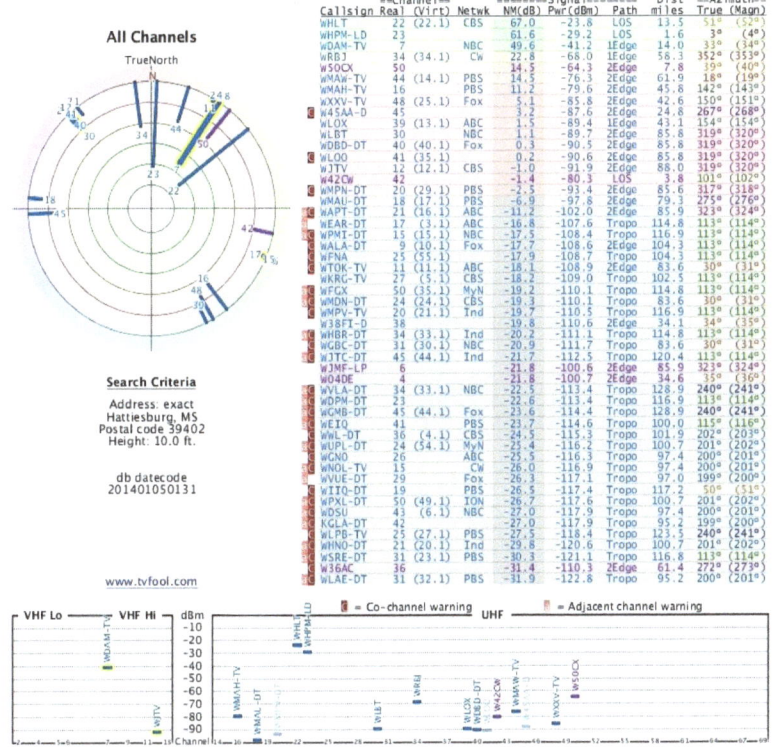

From TVFool.com

Advance: detailed list of stations and directions of towers

TVFool.com signal locator

Enter your address and height of antenna from ground level.

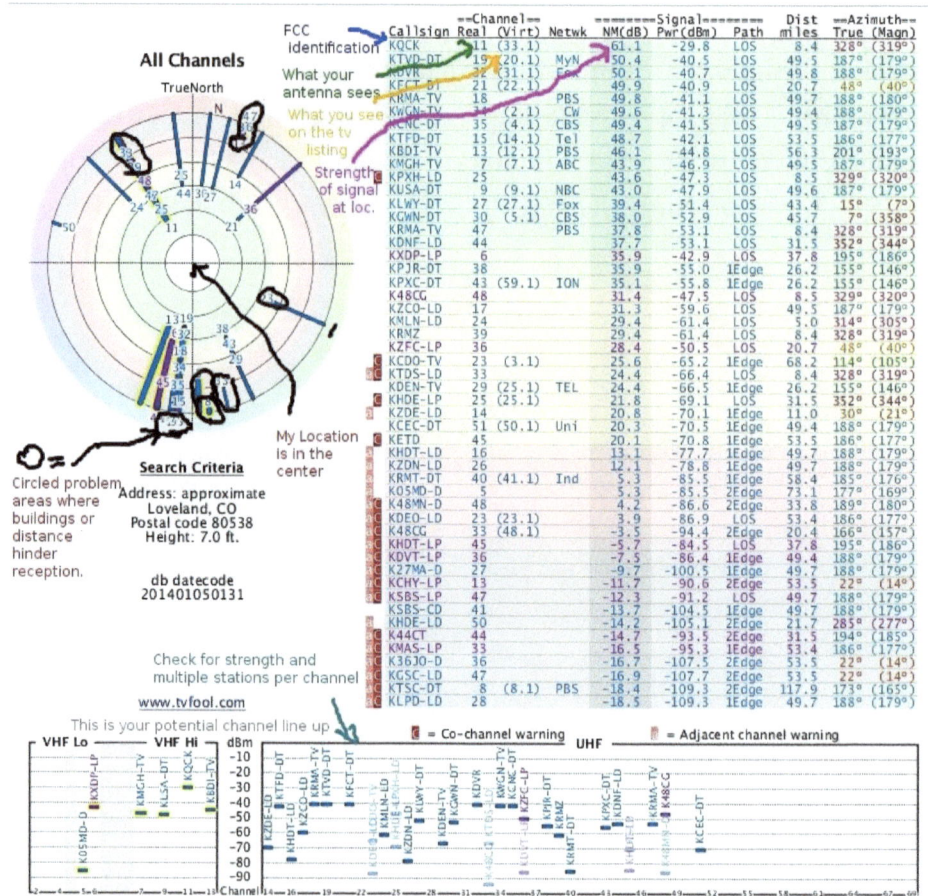

The Signal Analysis Report lists the broadcasters in your area, ranked from strongest to weakest, according to 3D of each transmitter in the table is color coded as follows:

Background color	Estimated signal strength
Green	An indoor "set-top" antenna is probably suffi
Yellow	An attic-mounted antenna is probably needed
Red	A roof-mounted antenna is probably needed
Grey	These channels are very weak and will most li

D) Sub channels (Rabbitears.info)(Best Quick Easy Overall Method - Shows sub channels)
Another quick way to see channels and start exploring HD sub channels is by using the map of the USA at rabbitears.info. This information will also be important if you set up a TitanTV program guide.

With the information gathered from the FCC and TVFool.com, you can now figure out most of the sub channels you may also receive.

1. Go to the following links depending on chosen method.

For a quick method

Go to http://www.rabbitears.info/search.php. Enter your Zip Code at a minimum. For a more precise information, enter your address. Enter your antenna height that you plan to use, for more accurate information. These results do not take into account obstacles such as buildings or hills.

For a visual method

http://www.rabbitears.info/market.php?request=marketmap

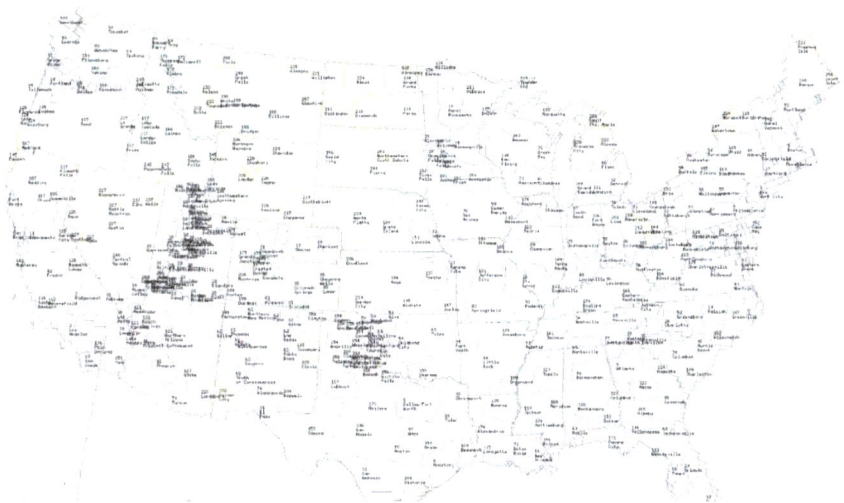

By Clicking on your market location, which you might have to locate using the pop-up label in crowded multi-viewing market areas, you will be given a list of TV channels originating and strongest within those areas. You may be able to receive stations outside this market area, but this is a good start.

2. Click on the market area you live in or are closest to.
3. *Expand All* to see a list of all the sub channels of these broadcasters.

In this example the WDAM (NBC) also transmits ABC, and Bounce TV. WMAH a PBS transmits 2 other channels: Create and MPB Music Radio. WHLT only transmits CBS. WHPM transmits FOX and CW. Digital channels can transmit up to 6 sub channels. Check with your local transmission towers to see what sub channels, besides the main channel (normally number 1 or 2) that you may pick up if you can receive and display that transmission tower's signal. The FCC page only shows the main channel.

It also gives information showing the video resolution. 480/I is SD. 1080/I is HD. Standard Definition (SD) and High Definitions (HD). Your TV must be able to receive 1080 resolution to gain the full feature effects.

Audio is either DD2.0 (2speaker) or DD5.1 (5 speaker plus subwoofer). Of course, you must have the appropriate audio equipment to hear the audio with the full feature effects.

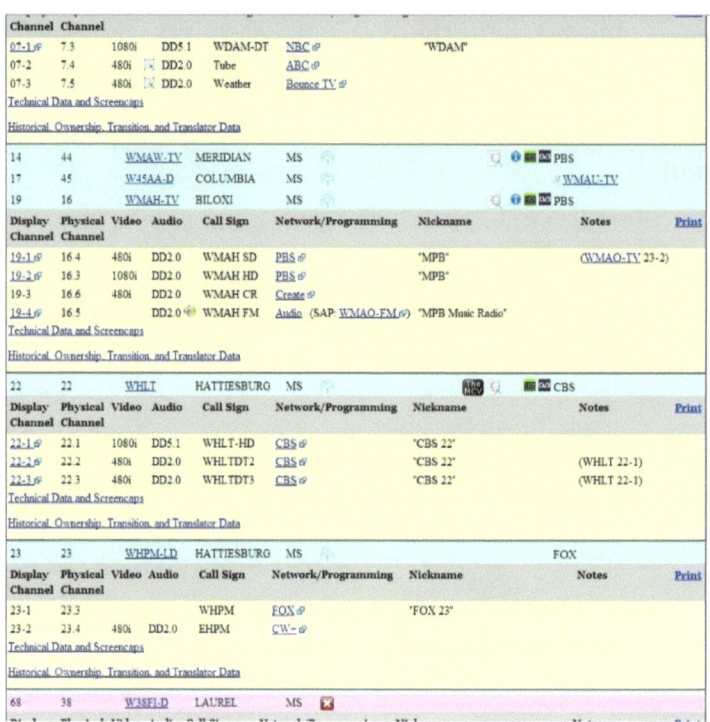

4. Go through the list of the different networks to see which networks you will receive. Here is a sample of the main networks from local TV towers in the close vicinity of Hattiesburg.

CBS [X] Chan _22.1-.3_ Dir_NNE__Dist_14 mi_ || Chan _____Dir_____Dist_____
ABC [X] Chan _7.2_Dir_NNE__Dist_14 mi_ || Chan _____Dir_____Dist_____
NBC [X] Chan _7.1_Dir_NNE__Dist_14 mi_ || Chan _____Dir_____Dist_____
Fox [X] Chan _23.3_Dir_N__Dist__2 mi__ || Chan _____Dir_____Dist_____
CW [X] Chan _23.4_Dir_N__Dist_2 mi__ || Chan _____Dir_____Dist_____
ION [ ] Chan _____Dir_____Dist_____ || Chan _____Dir_____Dist_____

Looking over this list lets me also know that I might not get ION TV station. I might check around other close viewing areas on Rabbitears to see if I might be able to pick up that channel from another close range source.

At the current time, there is also some online TV stations streamed off of sites or Filmon which can supplement and will be explained later. See those sections for further details.

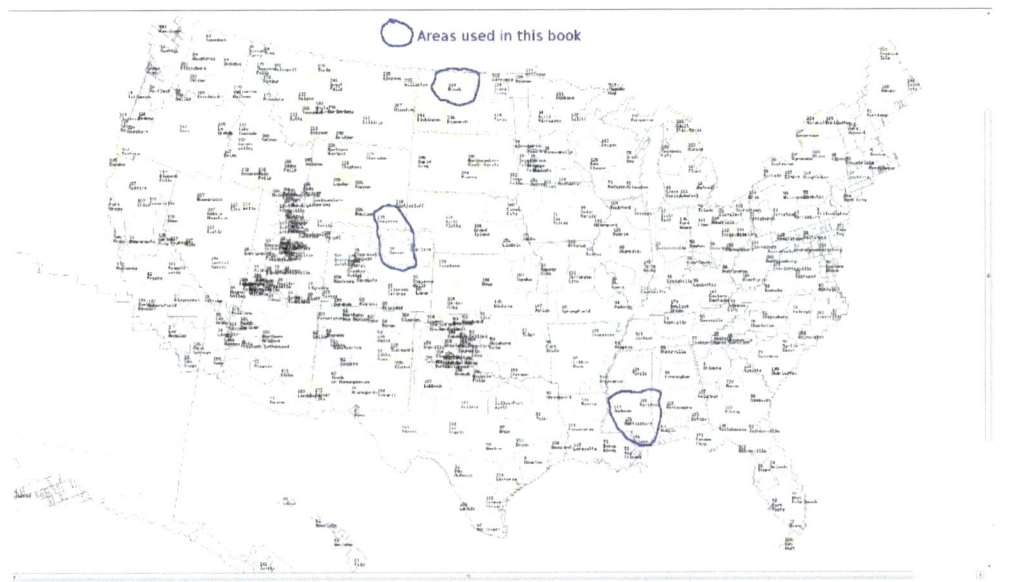

These are the areas that were checked with various tools in this book

These 3 viewing areas circled are the areas that Rabbitears covers in this book. Mississippi requires four different tower information. Colorado requires two. Antler required just one. Your viewing area may require several tower area information depending upon where you live and how many are near you.

Channel scan or auto scan

After your TV antenna is setup you need to scan for channels. Perform the following steps for most models. Read the TV instructions if these steps are insufficient.

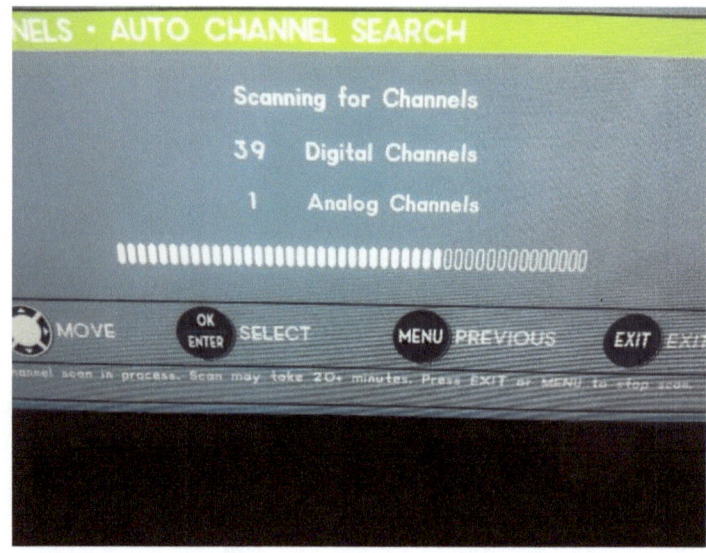

Auto scanning for channels

1. *Make sure all cable connects are secure and input devices are turned on.*
2. *Press the Input or TV button and make sure the TV is in TV input signal mode. The mode may also have an "Ant" or Antenna mode.*
3. *You may have to continually press input button to change to antenna or TV mode.*
4. *Open the TV or converter box onscreen Menu. Select TV or Tuner option.*
5. *In the Tuner option make sure the mode is antenna, if not change it.*
6. *Select Auto search, Auto scan, Auto Channel Scan or some variation to initiate the search for channels.*
7. *When the search reaches 100% exit and use the appropriate control channel + or – button to change the channel to see what channels you have found. Use the TV remote if directly connected to the TV. Use a converter or other device if connected to that device instead.*
8. *If problems persist factory reset the TV consulting the TV your TV manufacturer's website. Normally it is done by holding down the menu or power button from 15 to 30 seconds. You can also sometime find it in the Menu under System or Setup menu.*

Scan for additional channels

Most TVs also have the ability to scan for additional channels. This ability is useful in order to add new channels whenever you change the antenna direction.

TV Program Guide

Although there is a built in electronic program guide in converter boxes and digital receivers, Using a good TV programming guide can help recording programs, checking what is on or what programs are coming up. Next I review several potential program guide to over-the-air (OTA) channels. Two program guides are pretty good though not always exact.

Each method or type of program guide I give my overall reviews of pros and cons of each type of guide.

Guide to review of program guides

- Appearance – How visually appealing the TV program guide is
- Simplicity – Easy to use, ready to go
- Convenience – How easily the guide is to access the program information
- Registration – is site registration required to use
- Grouped program categories – does the TV program guide have the ability to look for programs by program type or categories

Photo of my TV Program **Info** button results

Pressing the Info button on my built in TV remote for antenna reception brings up the channel number, channel name, program name, episode summary, TV maturity rating, time, program length by time, and TV resolution. This TV does not have a very good built in TV program guide, rather a very basic one.

Built-in-electronic program guides (EPGs)

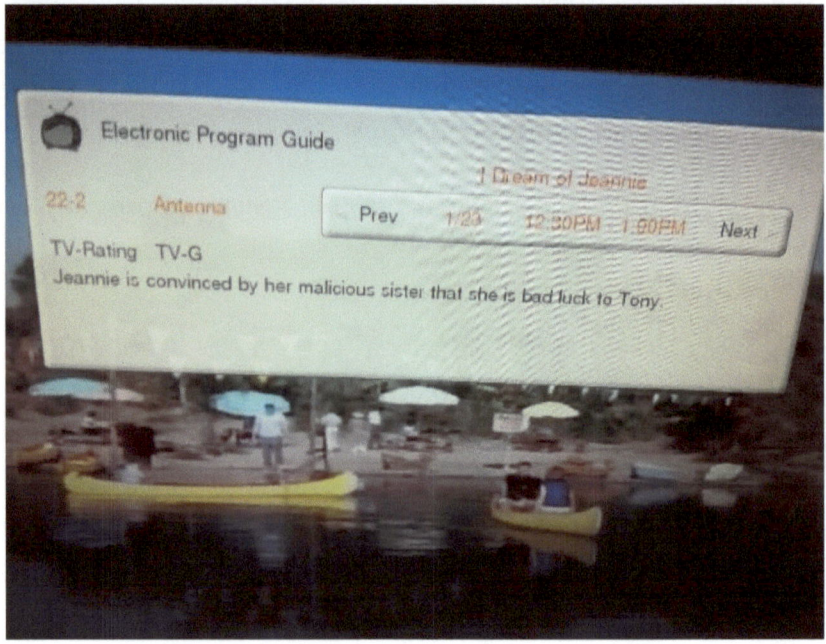

Photo of my TV **EPG** button results

Pressing the EPG button on my TV remote brings up a basic TV schedule for this antenna received channel, pressing right can show some upcoming program info. This TV is limited to

Most TVs, converter boxes, VCRs, media recorders, and computer media centers have some sort of build in program guide that shows channel shows, movies, and durations for current and upcoming content. These guides can be from a very limited time period of a few hours, to weeks in advance.

- Appearance – Varies from ok to great
- Simplicity – Most are very easy to use
- Convenience – Best Convenience. Since these are the built in to the TV, converter, software, or other receiving device, they are normally included with your main TV remote.
- Registration – No
- Grouped program categories – Not standard (some do, some don't)

Remote button normally designated to programming guide.

Accessing EPG is normally by the remote control by pressing guide, EPG, info, or some words along that kind of language. Some guides build into recordable devices VCRs and devices with hard drives have a record option.

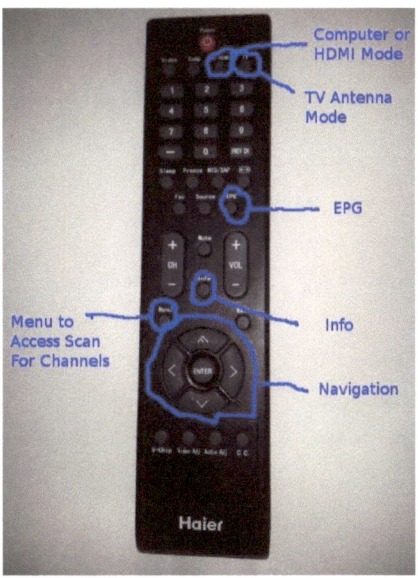

My TV remote

Navigating the guide is normally done by the arrow or direction arrows. You can normally check what is on other channels by scrolling up and down, or different times by side to side.

TVListings.AOL.com/ (Best for ready-to-go completeness)

My favorite ready to go listing is AOL's TV guide. This is powered by i.TV so it should be identical to iPhone and iPad App. If you register for a free AOL email account by just pressing the *EDIT CHANNELS* button, you can edit the channels removing unwanted listings. http://tvlistings.aol.com/

- Appearance – Great
- Simplicity – Very easy to use
- Convenience – Very Convenient
- Registration – Yes, to edit channels. No, if editing is not needed.
- Grouped program categories – Yes four groupings. Movies, News, Sports, Family.

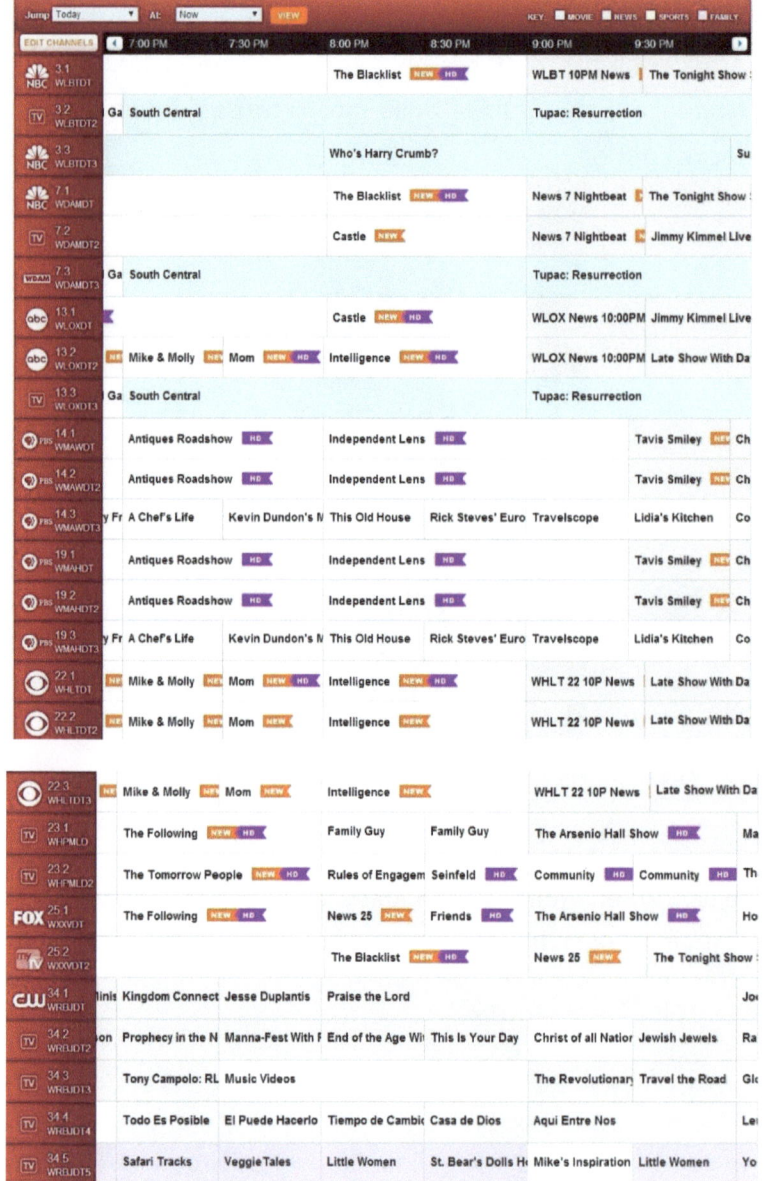

[TitanTV.com (Best for customization and details)](#)

Next TV program guide is TitanTV.com. Their guide needs a little more work to use. Once properly set up, it became one of my favorite TV program guides. I had to gather information from four different tower locations: Hattiesburg, Meridian, Gulfport/Biloxi, and a few from Jackson. It gets a little more confusing and time consuming. Each transmission area is on a separate page, so it is cumbersome. And it does not factor in confliction stations broadcast on the same channels. You can edit the Channels shown only by registering, whereas AOL is more of one stop info.

- Appearance – Very Nice when finished
- Simplicity – Complex

- Convenience – Somewhat convenient when completed.
- Registration – Yes, for customization.
- Grouped program categories – Twenty-one categories color coded. Key at the bottom.

This is a great tool after you already have an antenna and know what you can receive and what comes in. To use:

Add Broadcast Transmission Areas

1. Click the *ADD* button to create a new channel lineup.
2. Select the *Broadcast icon* to indicate that this is over-the-air transmission.
3. Enter your zip code.
4. From the drop down menu bellow your zip code, select your primary broadcast area.
5. Check the list and see if this list includes all of your receiving channels.
6. If not repeat the process, after your zip code, select another broadcast area that includes towers from a neighboring broadcast area that you receive.
7. Repeat this if necessary to include all broadcast areas your antenna receives signals from.

This process might result in many separate lists. When all are accounted for, it is time to combine data. You must register a free account to do this step.

Merge and Refine Broadcast Transmission Area Data

1. Click on the *MANAGE* button.
2. Look for the Broadcast area that has the majority of your channels that you receive.
3. Click on the *EDIT CHANNELS* button for that main area.
4. Hide channels that you do not receive or don't want program information.
5. Next click the *ADD CHANNELS* button on this same screen in the upper menu bars near the top of the channel list.
6. Choose the *Choose Channels to Add From an Existing Lineup* button.
7. Select the drop down menu down arrow.
8. Choose the next closest transmission area from the list, which you selected earlier.
9. From this list, select each of the channels that you receive which will turn green and show a (ADD) on the right. Don't add any that you do not receive nor want.
10. Click *ADD CHANNELS* button when complete.
11. Repeat process to add channels if more than 2 transmission areas, until all the channels represent what you receive.
12. You can also possibly add channels not listed in either if the information is available. I added EWTN because it was not listed in any transmission areas, although it is in our area, and I watch it occasionally. You can try ADD CHANNELs button then Find Channel to Add by Name. This may or may not work depending on available information. Or you

can try finding that channel in another transmission area, and add it to yours and see if it works.

With a little modification and configuration. Titan TV becomes the best TV program guide. Apps are available for iOS and Android devices. There is also a mobile version for other mobile device operating systems. Truly a powerful portable TV program guide.

Enjoy

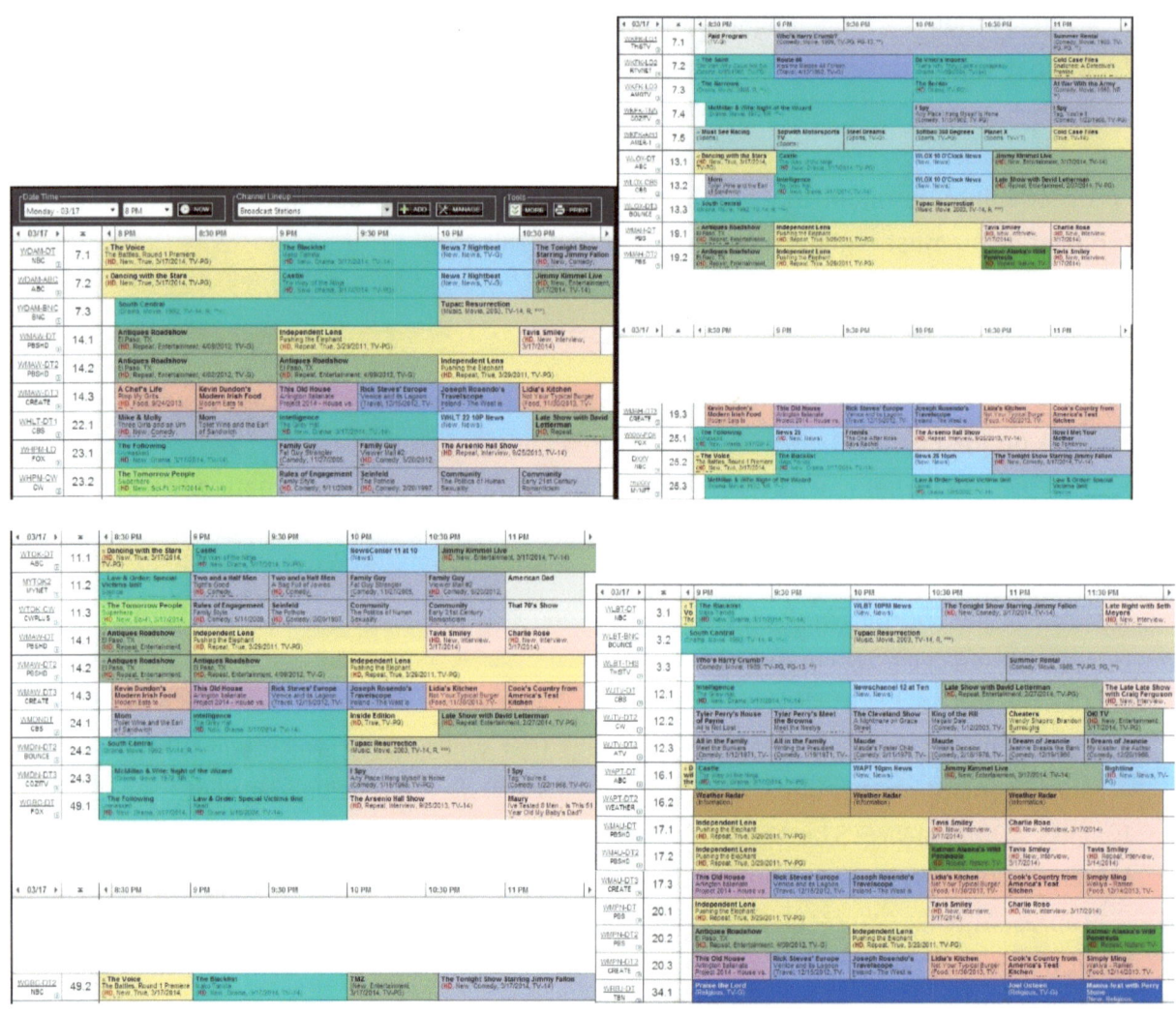

TV Guide (Most well known)

TV Guide does an ok job of bringing up the best channel, though it might miss the channels coming from further away. This guide has a tab system to keep track of movies, news, sports, family, and favorite shows. http://www.tvguide.com/

- Appearance – Plain, a bit boring.
- Simplicity – Easy to use.
- Convenience – Can be convenient.
- Registration – Yes for favorites and customization. No for as-is use.
- Grouped program categories – Five tabs; Movies, News, Family, and Sports. There also is a Favorites category.

Setting TV Guide up

1. You set it up by going to WHAT'S ON TV and then to TV LISTINGS.
2. Select the *Change The Location/Provider* link.
3. A popup will ask for your zip code. Enter your zip code and then select the *ANTENNA* button.
4. Select your Broadcast area such as *Denver Area Broadcast (Denver) (OTA Broadcast)*, which should appear after you enter your zip and select antenna.

iOS and Android devices have a TV Guide App you can install.

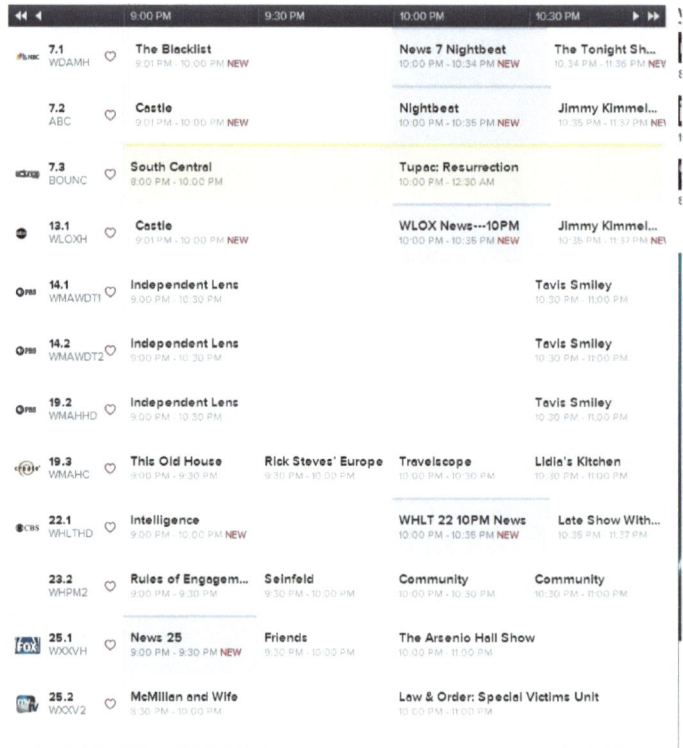

It has a tab system to keep track of movies, news, sports, family, and favorite shows.

Zap2It.com

Zap2It is similar to AOL's format, though not as colorful. I won't show all of it since it is long, filled with several ads. Yahoo uses Zap2It for its listings.

- Appearance – Very good
- Simplicity – Easy to use
- Convenience – Somewhat convenient
- Registration – Yes, for customization. No, for as-is use.
- Grouped program categories – Twelve categories called *Genres*. Just click to filter the desired categories.

Setting up your location and channel lineup
1. Change My Location
2. Enter zip code. Hit the GO button.
3. Select Local: Broadcast (Antenna)
4. You can change what channels are shown by removing ones you don't use by pressing the *Set Preference* link.
5. ADD only the channels that you watch. Repeat until you have a satisfactory list.

6. I like to check the **Additional Settings**: *Show Six Hour Grid* and *Show Only My Favorite Channels on the Grid settings*.
7. Optional: You can Display Description or Hide Description for a short summary of what each program contains.

Zap2It has a highlighter for favorites, sports, news, movies, and children shows.

- Select what types of programs you want highlighted

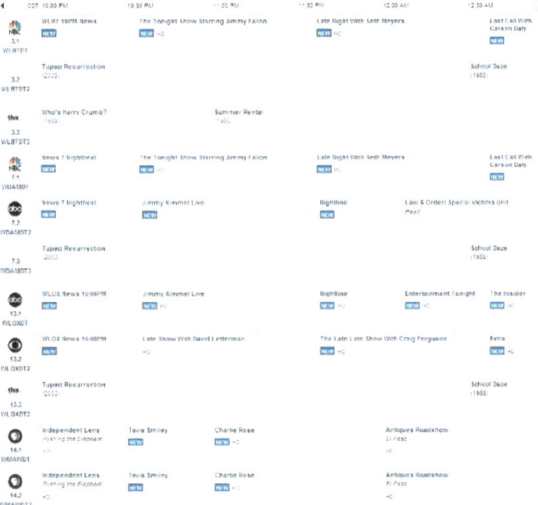

TV.com (Best for online streaming)

1. Click on LISTINGS menu heading.
2. A default area will pop up. Enter zip code. Click on the Choose Provider down arrow and choose a Broadcast TV, (Over-The-Air) appropriate.
3. You must have an account to hide channels and make favorites. To hide any channels hover over near the station number and icon. Select the "X" to any channels you want to hide. To favorite channels, do the same except select the heart symbol.

- Appearance – Similar to TV Guide.com
- Simplicity – Fairly easy to use
- Convenience – Someone convenient. Integration of show information and online viewing sources makes this service stand out among all others. This might be a favorite of online streamers.
- Registration – No
- Grouped program categories – Fourteen categories plus favorites.

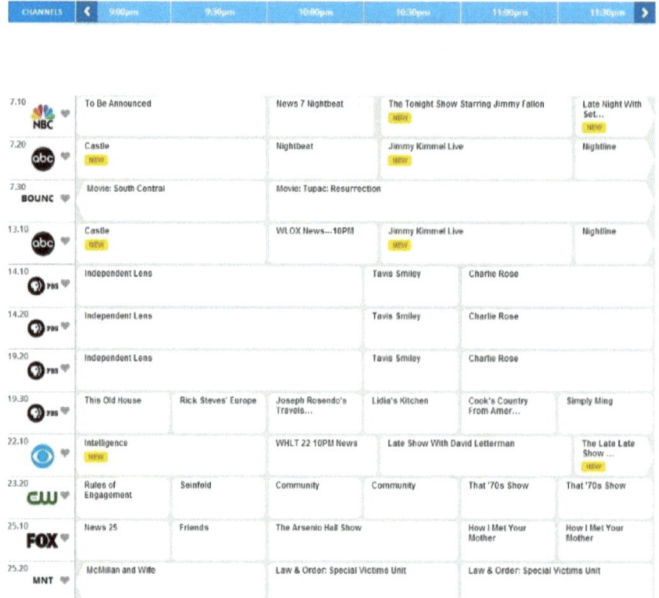

Results are a very similar to TVGuide.com except a little more colorful icons and NEW show indicator. It does not have any method to find types of TV shows, movies, news, nor sports like some of the others.

Windows Media Center

After connecting your antenna to your TV Tuner card you can open Windows Media Center, go to *TV*, and then go to *Live TV*. Normally if you have never used the service before it will start the set up to scan for channels. When this whole walk-through process is done, click on Guide to see the TV program guide.

If you have used the tuner before you may have to go to *Tasks> Settings> TV> TV Signal>*, then *Set Up TV Signals*.

Mobile Users
Check your app stores for available TV program guide apps.

Retailers that sell antennas

Store and online

Target www.target.com
Walmart www.walmart.com
Best Buy www.bestbuy.com
Radio Shack www.radioshack.com
Sears www.sears.com
Kmart www.kmart.com
Fry's www.frys.com

Home Improvement

Lowes www.lowes.com
Home Depot www.homedepot.com
Ace Hardware www.acehardware.com
Menards www.menards.com

Used

Goodwill www.goodwill.org
Salvation Army Family Stores http://satruck.org/national-family-stores
Search for local thrift shops http://www.thethriftshopper.com/

Online

Antennas Direct www.antennasdirect.com
Amazon www.amazon.com
New Egg www.newegg.com
EBay www.ebay.com
Overstock www.overstock.com
Rakuten www.rakuten.com
Think Geek www.thinkgeek.com
Crutchfield http://www.crutchfield.com/g_15920/TV-Antennas.html
Wineguard http://www.winegard.com/get-free-tv/
Clear TV (As Seen On TV 25 mile range) http://www.buycleartv.com/

Outdoor Antennas

Solid Signal http://www.solidsignal.com/
Channel Master http://www.channelmasterstore.com/
TV Antennas Sale http://www.tvantennasale.com/
Home Antenna http://www.homeantenna.org/

Basic TV Terminology

Electromagnetic waves

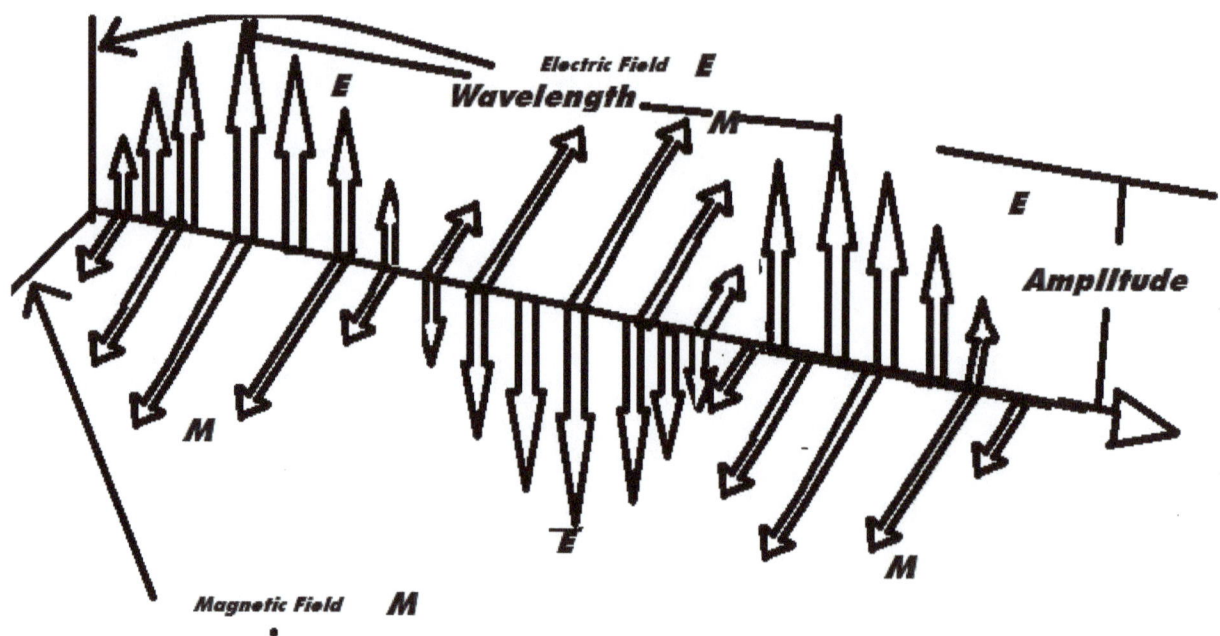

Drawing of electromagnetic wave by Ken Wickham

Antennas receive electromagnetic waves (EM) in specific spectrum. Our eyes see colors in the visual color spectrum. Radios pick up a specific spectrum of electromagnetic waves. These waves are electric fields travelling away from the source, the transmission tower. A magnetic field travels with the electric field thus making up the electromagnetic wave.

Speed of light = speed of electromagnetic waves

Both the speed of light and the speed of electromagnetic waves are roughly 671 million mph. The speed of sound is only 761mph at sea level, so the speed of waves is much faster than the speed of sound.

Sinusoidal Wave

Sinusoidal waves can be expressed by a combination of two axis of amplitude and either a) length or b) time.

Wavelength

Electromagnetic waves repeat themselves every meter (λ= Greek symbol Lambda). λ =   which means the wavelength equals the speed of light [c] divided by the frequency [v]. The speed of light per second is 186,212 miles/second.

Frequency

Electromagnetic waves repeat themselves every so often. Frequency (f = Latin F). T = time it takes to complete one cycle. Frequency is normally written in number of cycles per second called Hertz (Hz =)

Energy

Energy [E] equals Planck's constant [h] times frequency [v]. In the equation h is Planck's constant, h = 6.626 x 10-27 erg-seconds.

NETWORK TELEVISION (Online Website Links and Resources)

Commercial Television
*ABC   http://abc.go.com/   watch episodes
ABCNEWS   http://abcnews.go.com/   clips and news
*CBS   http://www.cbs.com/   watch episodes
CBSNEWS   http://www.cbsnews.com/   clips and news
*CW   http://www.cwtv.com/   watch episodes
*FOX   http://www.fox.com/   watch episodes
FOXNEWS (cable station)   http://www.foxnews.com/   clips and news
*NBC   http://www.nbc.com/   watch episodes
NBCNEWS   http://www.nbcnews.com/   news and clips

Public Telvision
*PBS   http://www.pbs.org/   full free episodes, news
CREATE   http://www.createtv.com/   schedule, episode info, clips, a few episodes
WILDTV   http://www.pbs.org/wnet/wildtv/
**MHZ   http://www.mhznetworks.org/   free full episodes, watch MHZ Worldview free live video streaming
*WORLD   http://worldchannel.org/   free full episodes mostly documentaries

Childrens
PBJ   http://watchpbj.com/ schedule
*PBS Kids http://pbskids.org/ schedule, clips, episodes
QUBO   http://www.qubo.com/home   clips, games

*BOUNCETV   http://www.bouncetv.com/ Some full episodes of original content, schedule
IONTV   http://iontelevision.com/   clips, schedule
MYTV   http://www.mynetworktv.com/   clips

Movies
THIS TV http://thistv.com/   schedule
GET TV   http://get.tv/   schedule
MOVIES! http://moviestvnetwork.com/ schedule
ESCAPE TV http://www.escapetv.com/ schedule

Music
**ZUUS COUNTRY   http://www.zuus.com/   watch free live TV stream

Living

IONLIFE   http://www.ionlife.com/ clips, schedule

*LIVING WELL   http://livewellnetwork.com/ watch many free episodes
MYFAMILY TV   http://www.myfamilytv.tv/ schedule
Tuff TV   http://www.tufftv.com/ full episodes of Auto Wars original programming

Classic TV

RETRO TV   http://www.myretrotv.com/ schedule
*ME TV   http://metvnetwork.com/ some free full episodes, schedule
ANTENNA TV   http://antennatv.tv/ schedule
COZI TV   http://www.cozitv.com/ schedule

Religious

**Atheist TV http://atheists.org/AtheistTV free live TV

**BUDDHIST (Buddhism)   http://www.thebuddhist.tv/   free live TV and radio stream

**BYUTV (Mormon)   https://www.byutv.org/   clips, episodes, free live TV
**CBN (Christian)   http://www.cbn.com/   clips, episodes, free live TV
**GODTV (Christian)   http://www.god.tv/   episodes, free live TV
**EWTN (Catholic)   http://www.ewtn.com/   news, information, live TV and radio stream

**ISLAM CHANNEL   http://www.islamchannel.tv/   news, information, live TV

**JLTV (Jewish Life)   http://www.jltv.tv/   show info, free live TV
**JN1 (Jewish News)   http://jn1.tv/   news, free live TV
**SHALOMTV (Jewish)   http://www.shalomtv.com/

*means full episodes are available

** means live streaming is available

Paid TV channels (Online Website Links and Resources)

*Has some free unlocked episodes.

**Has live streaming unlocked.

*A&E   http://www.aetv.com/   some full episodes, some locked, clips

ABCFamily   http://abcfamily.go.com/   watch live and episodes with TV provider permission

AHCTV   http://www.ahctv.com/   clips, schedule

AMC   http://www.amctv.com/   full episodes with TV provider permission, extras clips free

Al JEZEERA http://america.aljazeera.com/ clips

*Animal Planet   http://www.animalplanet.com/   some clips, newest finding bigfoot

Anime Network   http://www.theanimenetwork.com/ $6.95/month online

AXS TV http://www.axs.tv/ schedule

BBC America   http://www.bbcamerica.com/   some clips

BET   http://www.bet.com/   show clips and exclusives

*BIO   http://www.biography.com/   some full episodes, full biographies, and mini biographies

**BLOOMBERG   http://www.bloomberg.com/   free live stream USA, Europe, Asia, Event

*BRAVO   http://www.bravotv.com/   clips and some full episodes

**BYUTV (Mormon)   https://www.byutv.org/   clips, episodes, free live TV

**CBN (Christian)   http://www.cbn.com/   clips, episodes, free live TV

ChillerTV   http://www.chillertv.com/ clips, schedule

CLOO   http://www.cloo.com/   clips

*CMTV   http://www.cmt.com/   clips and some full episodes

*CNBC   http://www.cnbc.com/   many full episodes, watch live with TV provider permission

*CNN   http://www.cnn.com/   many clips by show, watch live with TV provider permission

*COMEDY CENTRAL   http://www.thecomedynetwork.ca/   full episodes of main shows

*COOKING   http://www.cookingchanneltv.com/home.html   recipes, watch some episodes

**CSPAN   http://www.c-span.org/   free Live CSPAN, CSPAN2, CSPAN3, CSPAN Radio, also clips

DESTINATION AMERICA   http://www.destinationamerica.com/   clips

*DISCOVERY   http://www.discovery.com/   many Mythbuster and other full episodes, clips

DISCOVERY FIT & HEALTH   http://www.discoveryfitandhealth.com/   clips

*DISNEY   http://disneychannel.disney.com/   some free full episodes, watch live with TV permission

E!   http://www.eonline.com/   clips and news

**ESPN   http://espn.go.com/   clips and news, Watch live ESPN3, Watch other ESPN with TV provider permission

ESQUIRE   http://tv.esquire.com/   watch live and episodes with TV provider permission

*FOX NEWS   http://www.foxnews.com/   clips and news, watch Fox News and Fox Business with TV provider permission

Fox Sports   http://msn.foxsports.com/   clips from shows

*FOOD NETWORK   http://www.foodnetwork.com/   many free full episodes

FUSE   http://www.fuse.tv/   clips

FUSION http://fusion.net/ schedule

*FX   http://www.fxnetworks.com/   clips and some free full episodes

FXX   http://www.fxx.com/   schedule

FXM   http://www.fxnetworks.com/fxm   schedule

G4   http://www.g4tv.com/   clips and news

*Golf Channel   http://www.golfchannel.com/   free full episodes, live with TV provider permission

*GSN (Game Show)   http://gsntv.com/   one of each full free episodes, clips

HALLMARK   http://www.hallmarkchannel.com/   clips

HALLMARK MOVIE   http://www.hallmarkmoviechannel.com/   schedule

*HGTV   http://www.hgtv.com/   many free episodes

*HISTORY   http://www.history.com/   many free full episodes

*H2 (History2)   http://www.history.com/shows/h2   many free full episodes

*HLN   http://www.hlntv.com/   clips and news

**HSN, HSN2   http://www.hsn.com/   all the shopping items, free live TV stream

*IDTV   http://www.investigationdiscovery.com/ full Episodes, clips

*IFC (International Film Channel)   http://www.ifc.com/   they have a free stream room

*LIFETIME   http://www.mylifetime.com/   some free full episodes, some with TV provider permission, some full lifetime movies

*LMN   http://www.mylifetime.com/movies/lifetime-movie-network   a few full episodes

*MLB TV & AUDIO   http://m.mlb.com/network   scores, news, registered user audio, subscriber video stream

*MSNBC   http://www.msnbc.com/   show clips, news, live with TV provider permission

*MTV   http://www.mtv.com/   news, clips, some full episodes, popular music videos

National Geographic   http://channel.nationalgeographic.com/   video clips, locked episodes

National Geographic Wild   http://channel.nationalgeographic.com/wild/   video clips

NBA TV   http://www.nba.com/nbatv/   clips, news, scores, league pass

NFL   http://www.nfl.com/nflnetwork   clips, news, scores, audio and video subscriptions

NHL   http://www.nhl.com/ice/eventhome.htm   clips, news, scores, subscriptions, archives

*NICKELODEON   http://www.nick.com/   many free full videos, games

*NICK JR   http://www.nickjr.com/   activities, games, video clips

*TOONS   http://nicktoons.nick.com/   many free full episodes, clips

OUTDOOR   http://outdoorchannel.com/   clips, info

OXYGEN   http://homepage.oxygen.com/   some clips, episodes with provider permission

OWN   https://www.oprah.com/own   clips

PALLADIA   http://www.palladia.tv/   just schedule

PIVOT TV http://www.pivot.tv/ clips, schedule

*POP TV http://poptv.com/ episodes, schedule

**QVC   http://www.qvc.com/   all the shopping items, free live TV stream

REELZ   http://www.reelz.com/   clips

REVOLT TV http://revolt.tv/ clips

**RT News (Russia Today) http://rt.com/ news, free live TV http://rt.com/on-air/

SCIENCE   http://www.sciencechannel.com/   clips

**SHOPHQ   http://www.shophq.com/   all the shopping items, free live TV streams

*SPIKETV   http://www.spike.com/   many free full episodes

*SMITHSONIAN   http://www.smithsonianchannel.com/   some full episodes

SPEED   http://msn.foxsports.com/speed   clips and news

SUNDANCE   http://www.sundance.tv/   watch with TV provider permission

*SYFY   http://www.syfy.com/   many free full episodes

TBS   http://www.tbs.com/   many full episodes and live with TV provider permission, Ground Floor without permission

TCM   http://www.tcm.com/   watch on demand and live with TV provider permission only

TENNIS   http://www.tennischannel.com/   clips, watch live with TV provider permission

*The Weather Channel   http://www.weather.com/   personal weather info, clips

*TLC   http://www.tlc.com/   a few full original series episode, clips

TNT   http://www.tntdrama.com/   live and episodes with TV provider permission

TruTV   http://www.trutv.com/   clips, episodes with TV provider permission

*CARTOON Network   http://www.cartoonnetwork.com/   some clip, 1 free episode no permission for 10 cartoon series, others require with TV Permission

*TRAVEL   http://www.travelchannel.com/   some free episodes and clips

TVGUIDE NETWORK   http://www.tvgn.tv/   some free full episodes, clips

*TVLAND   http://www.tvland.com/   many free full episodes

*TVONE   http://tvone.tv/   some full episodes

UPTV (formerly Gospel Music Channel)   http://www.uptv.com/music   clips and video

USA   http://www.usanetwork.com/   some free full episodes, most episodes with TV provider permission

VELOCITY   http://www.velocity.com/   clips

*VH1   http://www.vh1.com/   many free full episodes

WWE   http://www.wwe.com/   clips, news, WWE Network with subscription

HBO   http://www.hbo.com/   clips, HBO subscription coming in 2015

CINAMAX   http://www.cinemax.com/   clips

SHOWTIME   http://www.sho.com/   clips

The Movie Channel (owned by Showtime)   http://www.sho.com/site/tmc/videos/home.do

ENCORE   http://www.encoretv.com/   trailers and clips

*STARZ   http://www.starz.com/   free full <u>first</u> episode only of each series

NOTES